THE JOY OF ADVENT

THE JOY OF ADVENT

FAMILY CELEBRATIONS FOR ADVENT & THE TWELVE DAYS OF CHRISTMAS

Rebecca Grabill and Stephen Grabill, PhD

Illustrated by Clare Therese Gray

PARACLETE PRESS

Brewster, Massachusetts

2024 First Printing
The Joy of Advent: Family Celebrations for Advent and the Twelve Days of Christmas

Author is represented by the literary agency of Credo Communications LLC, Grand Rapids, Michigan, credocommunications.net

ISBN 978-1-64060-955-6
The Paraclete Press name and logo (dove on cross) are trademarks of Paraclete Press.

Library of Congress Cataloging-in-Publication Data
Names: Grabill, Rebecca, author. | Grabill, Stephen J., 1967- | Gray, Clare Therese, illustrator.
Title: The joy of Advent : family celebrations for Advent and the Twelve Days of Christmas / Rebecca Grabill and Stephen Grabill, PhD ; illustrated by Clare Gray.
Other titles: Family celebrations for Advent and the twelve days of Christmas
Description: Brewster, Massachusetts : Paraclete Press, [2024] | Includes bibliographical references. | Summary: "A celebration of Advent and Christmas that gives the whole family the opportunity to joyfully focus their hearts on Christ's love and on scripture"-- Provided by publisher.

Identifiers: LCCN 2023057398 (print) | LCCN 2023057399 (ebook) | ISBN 9781640609556 (hardcover) | ISBN 9781640609563 (epub)
Subjects: LCSH: Advent--Prayers and devotions. | Christmas--Prayers and devotions. | BISAC: RELIGION / Holidays / Christmas & Advent | RELIGION / Christian Living / Devotional
Classification: LCC BV40 .G69 2024 (print) | LCC BV40 (ebook) | DDC 242/.332--dc23/eng/20240220
LC record available at https://lccn.loc.gov/2023057398
LC ebook record available at https://lccn.loc.gov/2023057399

10 9 8 7 6 5 4 3 2 1

Published by Paraclete Press
Brewster, Massachusetts
www.paracletepress.com

Printed in India

TO OUR CHILDREN

Nicholas, Sebastian, Magdalene, Penelope, Kilian, and Emeric

You all are children of promise and you've been tightly wound in the scarlet cord of God's redemptive Love.

R.G. & S.G.

FOR

Liz, Liz, Liza, and their families

With our love x

C.T.G.

CONTENTS

INTRODUCTION

It was December 3rd, and I had yet to pull the Christmas bin from the basement closet. Inside languished our wooden Advent calendar, a festive red and white box with twenty-four numbered doors just the right size to stock wrapped holiday candies. We would be three doors behind *if* I pulled it out today.

Every year I enter the holiday season with grand intentions: I will teach every Christmas carol to the children! We'll bake cookies every day (and won't gain an ounce)! We'll read from a Jesse Tree devotional over a home-cooked dinner each and every night! We'll watch all the Christmas movies, and celebrate St. Nicholas Day, and . . .

The days in December fly by in a blur of parties, events, obligations, and more opportunities for activities than we could possibly attend or accomplish. All good things, true. *But each year I wish I'd given my children a more substantive understanding of the true meaning of Christmas.* I long for them to understand how Christmas has been celebrated in the past and what the traditions they know so well—like stockings and twinkling lights—*actually mean*. Every year I have ideas, links to recipes, crafts, movies, books, and songs I know the children would love, but the busyness of daily life pushes them to every *tomorrow's* to-do list.

Which leads me here. We began assembling this book years ago for ourselves and for our own family. We wanted to live each day of the Advent season with intentionality: to preserve our traditions, develop new ones, and provide our children (and ourselves) with meaningful holiday memories. We wanted to extend Christmas through Epiphany as did the early church. And we wanted our children to grow up knowing—*and understanding*—why we celebrate Christmas at all.

Now Stephen and I are absolutely delighted, in the true spirit of the holiday, to share our family's celebration with you. I pray that you will be blessed as you join our family in celebrating the rich and meaningful holiday seasons of Advent and Christmas.

—Rebecca Grabill

Rebecca Grabill

www.joyofadvent.com

When Does Advent Begin?

Advent officially begins on the fourth Sunday before Christmas. Since Christmas Day falls on different days of the week in different years, the first day of Advent likewise can fall anywhere from late November to early December. Since the start day varies, the actual length of Advent also varies. Because of Advent's variability and the constraints of a printed book (and busy families!), *The Joy of Advent* begins daily Celebrations on December 1st. The first Sunday of Advent may fall a few days after you've begun daily readings or a few days prior. Each year, check your calendar for that first Sunday or sign up for our emails online, and we'll send you a Sunday Supplement for each Sunday in the Advent season.

On each Sunday during Advent, one candle is lit, the wreath growing in brightness as Jesus's birth nears. The first Sunday we light the Prophet's Candle. This purple candle represents the HOPE of the prophets who foretold the birth of Jesus.

The second Sunday we light the Bethlehem Candle. This purple candle represents the coming PEACE as Mary and Joseph traveled to Bethlehem.

The third Sunday, called Gaudete Sunday, we light the Shepherd's Candle. This pink candle represents the JOY of the Shepherds upon hearing of Jesus's birth!

The fourth Sunday we light the Angel's Candle. This purple candle represents God's endless LOVE in the birth, life, death, and resurrection of Jesus.

On Christmas Eve and throughout Christmastide we light the Christ Candle. This white candle represents the purity of Christ, our sinless and loving Savior.

Girolamo Genga (1467–1551), A Jesse Tree *(ca. 1535), National Gallery, London*

A Jesse Tree by Girolamo Genga depicts the genealogical lineage of Jesus Christ in the Old Testament. The central figure is Jesse, father of King David, from whom Matthew recounts Jesus's descent. Around Jesse, various other biblical figures are portrayed, including David, Solomon, and other ancestors leading up to the Virgin Mary and ultimately Jesus Christ. The composition visually traces the ancestry of Christ, symbolizing the fulfillment of Old Testament prophecies in the New Testament.

About the Jesse Tree

The Joy of Advent: Family Celebrations for Advent and the Twelve Days of Christmas is structured around an ancient tradition based in Scripture.

> *There shall come forth a shoot from the stump of Jesse,*
> *and a branch from his roots shall bear fruit* (Isa. 11:1).

The first dated illustration of the Tree of Jesse is found in an illustrated manuscript, *Vyšehrad Codex* of Bohemia from the year 1086. It inspired countless illustrations and depictions in every artistic medium from stained glass and floor mosaics to reliefs, paintings, and more. It retold the story of God's plan for salvation to the ordinary people, many of whom could not read or write.

Originally the Jesse Tree depicted only persons in the family tree of Jesus, those people directly mentioned in the genealogies in Matthew and Luke, but over time it broadened to include stories and people who point the way to Jesus even if they're not directly in Jesus's lineage.

While most of the stories we've chosen for *The Joy of Advent* involve characters in Jesus's lineage, we, like more recent traditions, include some from outside his genealogy. All the events and figures were carefully selected because they or their stories point the way to Jesus with such beauty and power, we can't *not* share them.

Since our celebration continues throughout the Twelve Days of Christmas, rather than go back into history, we move forward to events and people important in Christ's early life. This structure is biblical and meaningful, and it provides a concrete way for even young children to discover God's plan for themselves and the world as it is revealed in the person of Jesus Christ.

A Jesse Tree Display allows the family to track the progression of Advent and Christmas so everyone can revisit the stories as new layers of meaning come throughout the season. Over the years, we've created ornaments with a symbol representing each day's figure. Our early Jesse Tree Display was a small faux Christmas tree and handmade ornaments. In recent years we've used a wire tree with lighted cherry blossoms. A Jesse Tree Display need not involve a tree at all. The printable ornaments available at our website could be part of a Jesse Tree Display that is hung with small clips on a cord over a window or doorway like a garland, or, a favorite for toddlers, attached to an empty wall with tape or putty. The one common element in all these display ideas is access—it's available for the whole family to enjoy, study, and remember.

DECEMBER 1

IN THE BEGINNING

Prepare Your Heart

(Teens & Adults)

Scripture: Genesis 1:1–10 & John 1:1–4

Personal Reflection: The artist sits before his canvas. He closes his eyes and imagines: a stream, a mountain, sunlight filtering through golden maples. He opens his eyes and . . .

What happens when we experience beauty? The photographer reaches for her camera, the artist picks up his brush, the family gathers on a winter walk. Beauty in their hearts creates memories of togetherness.

Creation, in a sense, is God's heart overflowing into the world. His goodness, his truth, his beauty, is so great, so full, it overflows and is part of everything. Because God created *ex nihilo*—from nothing—he bestowed his goodness onto every living thing. From nothing came everything.

In the beginning, "God said, 'Let there be light.'" He spoke the world into being. "In the beginning was the Word, and the Word was with God and the Word was God" (Jn. 1:1). Before the creation of the world, Christ was. He dwelled with the Father and the Holy Spirit in perfect unity, in an intimacy so close it transcended any human relationship. Yet it is this intimacy that models God's plan for all of us.

Advent is a season of preparation—and not just preparing gifts and festive dinners. Advent is a time to prepare our hearts for Jesus's birth and return. By preparing, we're creating habits that will yield rich memories and a deepened faith for us and our families. Let's take time to consider what our focus will be this Advent season. Relationships, faith, creativity, or something else? What is our intention, and why is that focus important?

Today consider setting up a Jesse Tree Display. See page xi.

Celebration!

(Families)

Focus Passage: *(Read aloud)* Genesis 1:1–2

In the beginning God created the heavens and the earth. The earth was without form and void, and darkness was on the face of the deep. And the Spirit of God was hovering over the face of the waters.

Jesse Tree Symbol & Description: What do you think of when you think of Jesus? You might think of Jesus as a baby in a manger. On Christmas Day we celebrate his birthday. But did you know Jesus was with God even when the world was created? Jesus *is* God, who came to earth as a tiny baby for a very important reason. That is why our first Jesse Tree symbol is God's beautiful world!

Today's Song: *Angels from the Realms of Glory,* by Scottish poet James Montgomery, was first published in 1816. Let us reflect on how the same angels who "sang creation's story" are joined by all creation in praising God the "Father, Spirit, Son."

Family Reflection: Imagine nothing.

No earth, no sky.

No sound, no air.

No day. No night.

It's hard to imagine nothing, isn't it? Even if we close our eyes, we still see something—shadows or swirls of light, or darkness.

But in the beginning, there was absolutely nothing, not even darkness. There was only God who was full of beauty, goodness, and love. He was like an artist with an idea in his mind of something beautiful—his masterwork.

But how would he make it? He had no paints, no clay. He had only himself—his goodness, his beauty, his love.

And his word.

So he spoke, "Let there be light!"

And his words became light!

Day after day, God spoke: Light, darkness, day, night. He spoke and made sky and earth, water and dry land. He spoke and formed the shining sun and moon and every twinkling star. He spoke and brought the swimming things forth from the water, sent flying things to the skies, and with his words, creeping crawling things filled his beautiful, green earth.

Finally, he made man and woman and filled them with his very own breath.

He looked at all he had made and saw that it was good.

Together Time: (*Discuss the following questions)*

- What is your favorite part of God's creation?
- Why do you think God created the world? *(Answers will vary, but discussion could lead to God's creativity and his love for all he has made.)*
- What is most important to *you* as we begin this Advent journey? Why?

PRAYER

We praise you, our Good Lord God.
We praise you for the sun and moon,
for earth who brings us fruits and vegetables,
for flowers that reflect your beauty.
Teach us to honor you by taking care of your creation. Amen.

—Adapted from The Canticle of Creation,
St. Francis of Assisi (c. 1181–1226)

DECEMBER 2

THE PERFECT COUPLE

Prepare Your Heart

(Teens & Adults)

Scripture: Genesis 3:1–7, 11–24 & Matthew 4:1–4

Personal Reflection: Oh, that crafty serpent who preyed on Eve's innocence! He earned the curse of crawling on his belly and eating the dust of the earth.

We often focus on Eve's fateful bite, but instead let's shift our vision to another young woman, generations after Eve, and to an infant cradled in Mary's arms.

Like Adam, the *first man*, her baby was First of his kind. The Only, in fact.

This baby boy was God in human form.

Many consider God a distant force, untouched by emotion, hardship, temptation. And yet because Christ was born into *full* humanity, he knows hunger and deprivation, humiliation, and depression. He knows the temptation of sweetly whispered words. When we suffer, God not only knows, but *he knows*. Our grief, our shame, our desires.

He knows us fully because he became one of us.

Jesus faced the same temptations as the first man and woman. But unlike Eve, Jesus did not bite.

He obeyed, as did the young woman who bore him.

Theologians call Jesus the *Second Adam*, or the second First Man.

As Eve's rebellion, expressed in a shared bite of fruit, brought the curse of sin *into* the world, Mary, through the "fruit of her womb" (Lk. 1:42) shares the very One to free us from the curse.

Yes, the first couple—Adam and Eve—condemned us, but Jesus, the *Second Adam*, born of Mary, frees us.

And so, through Christ we can be grafted onto his family tree with the sweet sap of his body and blood.

Consider preparing Moravian Spritz cookie dough. See page 41.

Celebration!

(Families)

Focus Passage: *(Read aloud)* Genesis 3:14a, 15 (NIV)

So the LORD God said to the serpent, "Because you have done this,
"Cursed are you . . .
And I will put enmity
between you and the woman,
and between your offspring and hers;
he will crush your head,
and you will strike his heel."

Jesse Tree Symbol & Description: Have you ever been hungry or cold? Have you ever been sick with a stuffy nose and sore throat? Adam and Eve never got sick, or felt hungry or cold, not until after Adam and Eve ate the forbidden fruit. Because they listened to the serpent, which was Satan's voice, and disobeyed God, many things changed. Illness, hunger, sadness, and suffering came into God's perfect world. When Jesus was born, because he was human, he may have felt cold and hungry, too. God wanted everything in the world he created to be perfect, and through Jesus, he will make it perfect again.

Today's Song: *In the Bleak Midwinter* was first a poem written in 1872 by Christina Rossetti. The bleakness of the world outside the Garden of Eden must have felt "hard as iron" to Adam and Eve. Meditate on the wonder of Jesus, God in flesh, who willingly entered our bleak world.

Family Reflection: So often we focus on Adam and Eve. We imagine the sweet syrup of disobedience dripping down Eve's chin as she handed the forbidden fruit to Adam.

Let's instead look at the serpent.

He was not a cursed creature, not yet, so Eve had no reason to fear him. In fact, he was likely beautiful. Lucifer (Satan's name before he rebelled against God) was an angel of light. His evil, both then and now, wears a mask of beauty.

When Satan whispered, "Did God really say . . .," Eve looked again at the tree. She saw that the fruit was beautiful and good for food.

Satan's words were like honey, but from a tongue tipped with poison.

Eve knew nothing of poison, of course.

So she and Adam took a bite. They broke God's trust and his heart.

When sin came into the world, pain and sorrow and death came with it.

The serpent was also cursed, but even in God's punishment, there is promise!

Eve's offspring—someone who would be born many generations later—will battle the serpent, God said, and will crush his head. Satan never expected a baby laid in a manger would one day conquer him.

Together Time: *(Discuss the following questions)*

Satan is a very good liar. Do you ever find it hard to know what is true or false?

- Look at Genesis 3:15. What does *enmity* mean? *(Having an enemy or being enemies.)*
- Who is the woman mentioned? *(Eve.)*
- Who is Eve's offspring? *(Offspring means children or descendants, so all people are Eve's offspring.)*
- How will Jesus "crush the head" (v. 15, NIV) of Satan? *(Even though it may seem like Satan wins when Jesus dies on the cross, Jesus is resurrected and defeats Satan!)*

PRAYER

Most merciful God,
we confess that we have sinned against you
in thought, word, and deed,
by what we have done, and by what we have left undone.
We have not loved you with our whole heart;
we have not loved our neighbors as ourselves.
We are truly sorry and we humbly repent.
For the sake of your Son Jesus Christ,
have mercy on us and forgive us;
that we may delight in your will, and walk in your ways,
to the glory of your Name. Amen.

—*The Confession of Sin,*
from the Anglican Book of Common Prayer
(Renewed Ancient Text)

DECEMBER 3

WATER COVERS THE EARTH

Prepare Your Heart

(Teens & Adults)

Scripture: Genesis 6:5–22; 9:11–13

Personal Reflection: Imagine a slow leak in a bottom compartment of Noah's enormous ark. See the water sloshing around a giraffe's ankles, rising up to its knobby knees.

Wood alone was not enough to keep a vessel that size afloat, so Noah was instructed to seal each gap, inside and out, with pitch, or in the original Hebrew language, *Kopher* or *Kaphar*.

Interestingly, the Hebrew word for pitch has several different meanings. The most obvious meaning was the resin that was used to make a vessel watertight. But *Kaphar* also means: *to atone*, *cleanse*, *placate*, *ransom*, *to cancel*, as in canceling a debt.

Kaphar was not only sticky, wood-sealing pitch, but also salvation from the waters of judgment. Because of sin, we all *ought* to be washed away with the wicked, as in Noah's day, but a Savior was raised on a cross of wood and sealed redemption with the *Kaphar* of his blood.

And so God chose Noah and his family to save humanity. They likely spent their days feeding animals and fixing tiny leaks as waves pounded against the sides of their ship. Any vessel with gaps, no matter how small, could potentially sink.

And so it is with the Christian life. Daily concerns—a spouse's thoughtless comment, a discouraging note, or the friend whose life seems so perfect—have the power to weigh us down and make us waterlogged by despair, envy, greed, sin.

They have the power to sink us.

What will be the pitch in our lives?

Celebration!

(Families)

Focus Passage: *(Read aloud)* Genesis 6:5–6, 8
The LORD saw that the wickedness of man was great in the earth, and that every intention of the thoughts of his heart was only evil continually. And the LORD regretted that he had made man on the earth, and it grieved him to his heart. . . . But Noah found favor in the eyes of the LORD.

Jesse Tree Symbol & Description: Can you imagine living on a boat full of animals for more than a year? It would be like living in a floating zoo! Would you be frightened? Noah might have been afraid of animals breaking loose or fires starting. Maybe he feared that the ark would spring a leak. But God protected him and saved his family from the flood that covered the whole earth. God promised to send a way to save *all* of us from the sin Adam and Eve brought into the world. He sent us Jesus as a tiny baby.

Today's Song: *Ding Dong Merrily on High.* George Ratcliffe Woodward set words to a sixteenth-century bar tune in 1924 to celebrate the ringing church bells. Imagine Noah's joy at that first step out of the ark and onto solid ground. It may well have felt as if the sky were "riv'n with angel singing"!

Family Reflection: Most of us know the story of Noah's ark—a boat, rain, and more rain, a dove, and an olive branch.

A promise and a rainbow.

It's as familiar as Jesus in a manger.

In fact, it's so familiar that nearly every culture on earth has a story like it.

We always remember the ark on the rising and falling waves and the rainbow of promise. But what parts of the story do we forget?

All was violence on the Earth. People took what they wanted when they wanted it, without caring about others. We might imagine a world of cheating, stealing, and lies like the lies of Satan in every mouth and his wickedness in every heart.

Imagine what it would take to break God's heart and make him regret making humankind.

Imagine how different Noah must have been from everyone else in the world to be the only one God chose to save.

And so, Noah was given a gift—an *impossible* task: to build a boat the length of twelve school buses, as tall as a four-story building, with nothing but hand tools.

Noah's ark was itself a miracle!

This miracle lifted Noah and his family out of the water.

The wicked world was washed clean of its sin, and Noah was saved in an ark made of wood.

Wood that also made a manger . . . and a cross.

Together Time: *(Discuss the following questions)*

- Of all the animals on the ark, which is your favorite? Are there any you wish Noah had left behind?
- Why did God choose Noah and his family to build the ark? *(Focus on how Noah's heart was different from the wicked hearts around him and how we are called to be different from the world.)*
- Why is Noah's ark a story to read during Advent? *(We remember Noah because he is in Christ's family tree, and because Jesus is the means through which we are saved from the destruction of the flood, just as through the ark God saved Noah and his family.)*

PRAYER

God of the spirits of all flesh, who has shown mercy to me
And has saved me and my children from the waters of the flood,
And has not caused me to perish as you did the sons of perdition;
For your grace has been great towards me,
And great has been your mercy to my soul;
Let your grace be lifted up upon my children,
And let not wicked spirits rule over them
Lest they should destroy them from the earth.
But bless me and my children, O God, that we may increase and multiply and replenish the earth.

—*The Prayer of Noah,*
adapted from the Book of Jubilees, *chapter 10, vv. 3–4*

DECEMBER 4

Number the Stars

Prepare Your Heart
(Teens & Adults)

Scripture: Genesis 12:1–3; 15:1–6

Personal Reflection: Before Abram gazed into the starry sky and tried to count the stars, God asked him to do another impossible task. He was told to leave home, family, prosperity, everything he had ever known.

God offered Abram a promise, saying, "And I will make of you a great nation" (Gen. 12:2a). Was it hope of greatness that spurred Abram's obedience? Or did the second half of the promise sway him, the *reason* behind the promise: "so that you will be a blessing" (Gen. 12:2b).

A great nation and a future blessing of the whole world would come through Abram.

A great nation did arise, Israel. But within Israel, kingdoms divided, decayed, and crumbled, until it was just another province of the expansive Roman Empire.

It would seem God had forgotten his promise to Abram, later called Abraham, and his descendants.

Yet in that insignificant province, many years later, an angel came to the most insignificant of all. Mary was a descendant of Abram, true, but she was far from "great" in the eyes of her community. Yet Mary's faith was greater than Abram's when she said, "Let it be to me according to your word" (Lk. 1:38).

Through Mary, God's promise to Abram was fulfilled. A kingdom was established—God's eternal Kingdom—which will include all tribes and nations, and it will have no end.

The promise of blessing was fulfilled not through earthly greatness, but through willing, faith-filled, human hearts.

Let us all say, with Abram and Jesus's mother, Mary, *"Yes,"* as we offer ourselves to be God's blessing to the world.

Celebration!
(Families)

Focus Passage: *(Read aloud)* Genesis 15:4–5
And behold, the word of the LORD came to him: "This man shall not be your heir; your very own son shall be your heir." And he brought him outside and said, "Look toward heaven, and number the stars, if you are able to number them." Then he said to him, "So shall your offspring be."

Jesse Tree Symbol & Description: Yesterday we learned about Noah, who bravely obeyed God. Abram also obeyed God. God told Abram to pack up his whole family and move far away, and Abram did what God said. Would you ever want to move to a different house, city, or country? You might feel very small and alone. Abram may have felt that way, too, until God showed him the starry sky. God promised that Abram would have more children than the uncountable stars! We can always obey God, because God will always follow through on his promises.

Today's Song: *Creator of the Stars of Night*, translated by John Mason Neale in 1852 from a seventh-century Latin hymn, traces all of salvation history. Could Abram even imagine that the "medicine" for the ancient curse would be among the stars of his descendants?

Family Reflection: Come, let's look up at the stars. Can we count them, as they twinkle and dance behind clouds?

Even on the clearest night we can count just over 9,000, and we know there are far, far more. Trillions. More than trillions.

We live in a "prove it" world. A friend says, "I can count the stars," and we say, "Prove it!" A scientist says, "I can visit the stars," and we say, "Prove it!"

Abram left his home to travel the wilderness with his wife and their servants.

Why?

Because God promised. God said he would make Abram a great nation.

There was one problem. Abram had no children.

How could God possibly keep his promise?

And then, late one night, with a cool breeze brushing Abram's cheek, God took him outdoors. God told him to look up into the starry sky. And when God promised this childless man that his descendants—his children's children—would outnumber the stars, Abram did the unthinkable.

He believed.

He had no children, no proof. Yet he believed.

The Apostle Paul wrote in 1 Corinthians, "For the foolishness of God is wiser than men" (1:25a). Abram followed his faith with obedience.

When God says, "Trust, believe, go," what will we answer?

Together Time: *(Discuss the following questions)*

- What did God ask Abram to do? *(Answers could be: look into the sky, leave his homeland, count the stars, etc.)*
- Talk about blessings. How was Abram's "child," his descendant Jesus, a blessing to all nations?
- Do you believe in things you can't see, or do you need proof?

PRAYER

Make us, O Lord, obedient to your commandments, for then all things will go prosperously with us, if we follow the Author of our whole life, Jesus Christ. Amen.

—Adapted from Ancient Collects, *William Bright, 1902*

DECEMBER 5

SHE LAUGHS

Prepare Your Heart

(Teens & Adults)

Scripture: Genesis 18:1–15 & Hebrews 11:1–3

Personal Reflection: How many types of laughter can we name? We might list: a scornful laugh, a joyous laugh, a mocking laugh, a mirthful laugh. Have we ever laughed in amazement? In disbelief?

Imagine wishing for something our entire lives, so long we have abandoned hope that this thing, whatever it might be, would become ours.

What if we learned that this wish, this dream, would soon become a reality?

We might laugh—with the laughter of longing, of hope past all hope!

Sarah stood in the women's side of the tent, listening to her husband, Abram (renamed Abraham), and the other men beyond the flap. She heard the promise and shook her head with a sad smile. *This old body carry a baby? Now that would be something!*

God had promised, she knew, yet she had waited so very long and had tried to fulfill God's promise with her own wit—a son of Abraham born to her servant—and had added heartache to heartache.

But neither impatience nor striving in her own wisdom influenced God's faithfulness.

Advent is a time of waiting. We may even be in a time of waiting now—a prodigal child, an achingly empty womb, hope for an end to loneliness or illness.

As we wait during this season, let us remember the promise given to Abraham, that through him, all the peoples of the world would be blessed. And let us all celebrate Sarah's laughter when a Savior rescues a world past all hope!

Tomorrow is St. Nicholas Day! See page 27.

Celebration!

(Families)

Focus Passage: *(Read aloud)* Genesis 18:12–15
So Sarah laughed to herself, saying, "After I am worn out, and my lord is old, shall I have pleasure?" The Lord said to Abraham, "Why did Sarah laugh and say, 'Shall I indeed bear a child, now that I am old?' Is anything too hard for the Lord? At the appointed time I will return to you, about this time next year, and Sarah shall have a son." But Sarah denied it, saying, "I did not laugh," for she was afraid. He said, "No, but you did laugh."

Jesse Tree Symbol & Description: What sorts of things make you laugh? Sarah stood inside her tent, listening to Abraham and the other men talking. She laughed because she heard news that was too good to be true. Except it was true! Special visitors said that Sarah would have a baby. She thought she was too old to have a baby, but with God, all things are possible. Sarah's son, Isaac, was a gift from God. And his name means laughter!

Today's Song: *The First Noël* can be traced to either ancient Celts or Britons of the 1400s, the word *Noël* (or *Nowell*) meaning *Christmas*. Reflect on Abraham and Sarah's long journey guided by faith and the Magi's travel guided by a star. At the end of both journeys was the blessing of a child!

Family Reflection: Why did Sarah tell a lie?

We might answer that question with another question: Do you know how many words there are for "sea ice" in the Inuit language?

Ninety-three!

Let's look again at Sarah's response to the visitors' promise. "*So Sarah laughed to herself. . . .*"

She stood hidden in another part of the tent. Their visitors couldn't possibly hear her silent, *inward* laughter. So how did they know that she laughed?

Sarah understood, and she *feared.*

Let's think about the word *fear*.

In the Bible's original language, words sometimes have more and differing meanings, like "sea ice" in the Inuit language.

Sarah's *fear* wasn't the same as being *scared*. Her *fear* was amazement.

Only God could have heard the laughter of her heart.

And so, Sarah realized that their visitors were not ordinary visitors. They were sent from God.

By saying, "I did not laugh," Sarah is actually saying, "You are a messenger from God, and I believe!"

Sarah's amazement, her *fear* is a sign of faith (Heb. 11:11).

When her son is born one year later (as promised!) she will name him Isaac, which means *laughter*. Her laugh of amazement will become a laugh of joy to share with the world.

Together Time: *(Discuss the following questions)*

- What news did Abraham and Sarah's visitor bring? *(That God would give them a child, so the promise that Abraham would become a great nation would be fulfilled.)*
- Why do you think Sarah laughed when she heard the news? Would you have laughed?
- Have you ever laughed at something "impossible" God promised or did in your life?

PRAYER

Merciful Lord, our Comforter and Teacher, increase in your Church the desires for and hope in yourself by enabling us to understand. Show us the depth of your promises, that all of us, your adopted children, may even now see with eyes of faith, and patiently wait for, the light which you are about to show us! Through Jesus Christ our Lord. Amen.

—Adapted from Ancient Collects, *William Bright, 1902*

DECEMBER 6

A RAM IN THE THICKET

Prepare Your Heart

(Teens & Adults)

Scripture: Genesis 22:1–17

Personal Reflection: Before Sarah's laughter became a living, joyous child, Abraham listened to his wife's fearful pleading and agreed to take her servant, Hagar, as his wife. Ishmael, son of Hagar, was Abraham's firstborn, yet he was not the son of promise. He was the child of Sarah's impatience and her human efforts to fulfill God's promise in *her* time and *her* way, through *her* wisdom, rather than God's.

Perhaps Abraham regretted his choice to follow Sarah's lead, as Adam no doubt lamented his bite of fruit. Surely Abraham regretted the doubt that preceded Ishmael's birth, because when we meet him again here, facing this impossible command to sacrifice his son, Ishmael and Hagar are gone, cast out into the desert. Isaac was at least an older teen (some scholars even place him in his thirties!), and since Sarah was well past the "way of women" when Isaac was born, the thought of having *another* son? Unimaginable.

Isaac is Abraham's only heir, his only hope.

Surely Abraham had expectations for his son's future, yet he was willing to sacrifice those expectations to see God's purpose accomplished. We all tend to grasp onto our hopes with white-knuckled intensity, like Sarah, who connived her *own* way for God to fulfill his promise. We do the same with our fears, clinging to them, because by holding on we (incorrectly) believe we can control them.

Consider today: are we willing to sacrifice our expectations for the future on the altar of faith?

Today is St. Nicholas Day! See page 27.

Celebration!

(Families)

Focus Passage: *(Read aloud)* Genesis 22:13–14a (NKJV)
Then Abraham lifted his eyes and looked, and there behind him was a ram caught in a thicket by its horns. So Abraham went and took the ram, and offered it up for a burnt offering instead of his son. And Abraham called the name of the place, The-LORD-Will-Provide.

Jesse Tree Symbol & Description: Do you remember the story of the starry sky? God promised Abraham that he would have more grandchildren, great-grandchildren, great-great-grandchildren, and beyond, than the stars in the sky. Now God is asking Abraham to kill his son! How could God do what he promised if Abraham had no children at all? Abraham didn't know *how* God would keep his promise, but he knew God *would* keep his promise. God always keeps his promises. He thought God would even raise Isaac from the dead and make him alive again. But God had another way. He provided a ram, a male sheep. Many years later God let his Son die, and then made him alive again because of his love for us.

Today's Song: *It Came Upon the Midnight Clear*, written in 1849, followed a time of personal pain for Pastor Edmund Sears. Imagine the "crushing load" carried on the hearts of Abraham and Isaac as they ascended the mountain, and their joy as release came "swiftly on the wing."

Family Reflection: Many people wonder why a loving God would tell Abraham to kill his own child. We think so much about *what* Abraham was called to do that we forget to wonder about *why*.

Abraham was not being asked to partake in a human sacrifice, which happened often in Abraham's time. Rather, God was testing the faith of Abraham and Isaac both.

Remember, Abraham was already an old man when Isaac was born. Now Isaac was in his prime. Most Bible experts believe he was about twenty, twenty-five, or even thirty years old. Plus, Isaac was strong from having lived the life of a herdsman.

Frail, old Abraham could not kill a strong young man.

Let's think about Isaac.

He *allowed* himself to be tied up with ropes. He *allowed* his father to place him on an altar.

Imagine that sort of faith! Abraham and Isaac both believed in the promise of God so fully that they *knew* God—if needed—would raise Isaac from the dead to fulfill his promise.

As we prepare our hearts for the birth of Christ, let us remember Jesus, God's own Son, who was also a *willing* sacrifice.

Together Time: *(Discuss the following questions)*

- If you were Isaac or Abraham, what would you do?
- Why do you think we're reading this story during Advent? *(Answers will vary; bring discussion around to how Isaac's willingness to be a sacrifice mirrors Jesus's laying down his life for us.)*
- Think of a current trial, longing, expectation, or disappointment in your life that weighs on your spirit. You may have tried many ways to change or achieve or avoid this thing. How can you *let go and let God*?

PRAYER

Look on us, O Lord, and let all the darkness in our souls vanish before your light. Fill us with your love and wisdom. You know our deepest desires. We pray you will turn our hearts so we might long to seek your face and know you better. Grant us peace. Amen.

—Adapted from St. Augustine (354–430)

CELEBRATE
ST. NICHOLAS DAY

We've all heard of Santa Claus, sometimes called St. Nick, but who was the real St. Nicholas?

Long, long ago, in Patara (now Demre, Turkey), a husband and wife prayed fervently for a child. Years passed, and their prayers continued as they gave away much of their wealth so they would not love money and things more than God. At long last, the Lord gave them a son, Nicholas.

As Nicholas grew into a young man, he also grew in faith. He became a priest, giving his whole life over to serving God. When his parents died, Nicholas inherited their riches. He began giving money away to the poor in Patara.

It was then that Nicholas heard about a man in Patara who had suddenly become desperately poor. This man's three daughters were all old enough to marry, but their father could hardly scrounge together money to feed them all. He could never afford for them to marry. (During this time in history, a young woman's family gave an expensive gift called a dowry to the husband-to-be's family.)

According to legend, Nicholas tucked three small packages in his cloak, and in the darkest part of night, he slipped through the streets to their house. He stopped outside an open window, not knowing that the girls had earlier washed and hung their stockings there to dry.

While the household slept soundly, Nicholas took the packages from his cloak and dropped them through the window: three small bags of gold, each one landing in one of the girls' stockings. When the girls awoke the next morning, they and their father praised God. They had enough money to marry and some extra besides.

Nicholas continued to serve and help the poor, just as Jesus had served the people he loved so well. Today, many of us hang stockings as Christmas decorations, but few of us know the *true* story of the Christmas stocking, nor of St. Nicholas, giver of gifts, who so blessed the poor widower of Patara.

Tradition of the Shoes

On the Eve of St. Nicholas Day our children don't need to be reminded—they rush to place their shoes in a neat line by the front door. The next morning they sprint to see what St. Nicholas left for them.

- On the eve of St. Nicholas Day, line up one pair of shoes from each member of the family in a convenient location. Traditionally shoes are placed by a door, but any spot will do. If you forget the night before, that's okay! Fill shoes at any point on St. Nicholas Day.
- Fill shoes with treats. If this tradition is new, you may have to direct children to "check your shoes" and explain that the gifts are from St. Nicholas. You may tuck your letter from St. Nicholas in with their gifts, or wait until your family *Celebration*.

Supplies:

- 1 pair of shoes from each member of the family (adults too!)
- treats of your choice (ideas include a tangerine or an orange, gold chocolate coins, toy coins, small toys, new socks, candy canes, a special ornament for the Christmas tree)

Tiny Tot Tip: Toddler shoes are very easy to fill with treats, and their delight will be just as big as that of older siblings. They might receive a card picturing St. Nicholas with a prayer of blessing and a simple letter.

St. Nicholas Letters

Another favorite tradition is the St. Nicholas Letter. Also originating in Europe, according to tradition, St. Nicholas writes a letter to each child of the household praising them for their growth in the previous year and gently urging them to reflect on how they might improve. Children may then write back a reflection on how they intend to change, and, of course, they add their wish list.

- Use the printable St. Nicholas Letter template on the Joy of Advent website, or write a letter to each child. Be sure to include the following: 1. Praise for things St. Nicholas would love and appreciate about each child such as their maturity, kindness, or other admirable qualities. 2. Words of blessing for the coming year. 3. One small thing St. Nicholas would like to see improved upon, such as being a peacemaker in the family or strengthening a positive character trait. Be sure to add the date! Children often keep and treasure their St. Nicholas letters for years to come.
- Whenever you share today's *Celebration*, read the St. Nicholas story and encourage children to write letters back to St. Nicholas.

Supplies:

- a letter for each child from St. Nicholas
- paper and supplies for letter-writing

DECEMBER 7

BETWEEN HEAVEN AND EARTH

Prepare Your Heart

(Teens & Adults)

Scripture: Genesis 28:10–17 & John 1:51

Personal Reflection: Newborn Esau, ruddy and rugged, wailed his way into the world, followed instants later by his twin. Patient, quiet, determined, Jacob was born gripping his brother's foot.

Jacob was not going to be a man ruled by passions like his brother. No, through his patience and cunning he would grasp what Esau didn't respect more than a bowl of stew—the inheritance of the eldest son.

Later, while fleeing his brother's outrage, Jacob had a vision of heaven and earth connected, the gulf between humanity and heaven bridged.

There was a different, earlier group of people who built a tower in their attempt to reach God (the Tower of Babel, Genesis 11). They were scattered, just as Jacob was forced to flee his home, his father's riches, and the very inheritance he so desired.

Despite his cunning and deceptions, Jacob was given the same promise given to Abraham. Yet, why?

Jacob is another early member of a litany of similarly flawed saints—people God chose to use in spite of their humanity and faithless moments. Abram lied about Sarai, telling local rulers she was his sister rather than his wife, not once, but twice. And Sarah's own impatience led to a rival heir, Hagar's son Ishmael.

Jacob had traits that Esau lacked. The patience to wait, the willingness to obey, and most importantly—recognition of the value of his inheritance.

And so Jacob dreamed.

He discovered he could not *take* the promise given to his grandfather, Abraham, but it could be gifted. Likewise, we can never build a stairway, ladder, tower, or rocket that can reach God. But God can—and did—come down and give himself to us.

Celebration!

(Families)

Focus Passage: *(Read aloud)* Genesis 28:12

And [Jacob] dreamed, and behold, there was a ladder set up on the earth, and the top of it reached to heaven. And behold, the angels of God were ascending and descending on it!

Jesse Tree Symbol & Description: Do you ever remember your dreams? Jacob had a very strange dream, didn't he? A ladder went from the ground all the way up to God in heaven. Years and years before Jacob, all the people of the world tried to build a tower to heaven. Nobody can build a tower or a ladder tall enough to reach heaven. We can't climb to heaven, but when Jesus was born, God came all the way *down* to earth to be with us. Jesus is like Jacob's ladder—Jesus is the only ladder between heaven and earth.

Today's Song: *Angels We Have Heard on High* was paraphrased by James Chadwick in 1862 from an eighteenth-century French Christmas carol. Picture the unimaginable distance between angels "on high" and even the highest mountain. Only Jesus could bridge that impossible divide.

Family Reflection: Imagine going to sleep in an open field. Sometime during the night, a dream comes. . . .

A ladder appears, covered in glittering angels, dropped down from heaven.

How far away is heaven? We often think of heaven being in the sky, perhaps in the stars. With modern technology we know it would take more than 80,000 *years* to reach the nearest star.

What if heaven isn't *actually* in the stars?

For Adam and Eve, heaven was the garden, not because of its beauty, but because it was where they could walk and talk with God. When Adam and Eve sinned, the relationship was broken. Heaven was now more distant than the *farthest* star.

Scholars have wondered at Jacob's strange vision since the writing of the Torah (the first five books of the Bible). They still talked about it while Jesus, as a child, sat listening in the temple.

Later, the adult Jesus would say, "Very truly I tell you, you will see 'heaven open, and the angels of God ascending and descending on' the Son of Man" (Jn. 1:51, NIV).

We cannot reach God, but God can *and did* reach a ladder down to us, sung by choirs of angels, more than two thousand years ago.

Together Time: *(Discuss the following questions)*

- Can you describe Jacob's dream?
- How far away is heaven? *(Discuss how heaven is dwelling with God and that we can't reach God without Jesus.)*
- It seems unfair for God to give the inheritance (and promise of blessing for Abraham) to the younger brother. Why do you think God did this? *(Answers will vary; guide discussion to Jacob's appreciation for his inheritance and how God repeatedly turns our expectations upside-down.)*

PRAYER

O Lord our God, who came down for the salvation of mankind, look upon us, your servants and inheritance. For to you we bow, waiting for your pardon and salvation. Guard us at all times from every foe, from every adverse working of the devil, from idle thoughts and wicked imaginations. Amen.

—*Adapted from Vespers of Eastern Church in* Ancient Collects, *William Bright, 1902*

DECEMBER 8

THE DREAMER'S COAT

Prepare Your Heart

(Teens & Adults)

Scripture: Genesis 37:3–8, 19–28; 45:4–8

Personal Reflection: Who wouldn't long to be the favored child? Joseph had what his father, Jacob (now called Israel), lacked: a father's favor. And as proof, Joseph had a magnificent robe with sleeves to his wrists, and stripes or patches wide as his hand. Kingly, this robe.

Oh, how his brothers seethed—the youngest, already doted upon by their father, was now wearing their inheritance! A robe was not *just* a garment, not then. In Joseph's day, a robe was often passed down from father to son, to his heir.

This robe showed more than inheritance. It showed blessing, and with it a whisper of royalty—royalty which Israel would not see for generations. The only other instance of this particular type of robe, *k'tonet pasim*, is in the story of Tamar. We learn that "this was the kind of garment the virgin daughters of the king wore" (2 Sam. 13:18, NIV).

Watch Joseph ride out to where his brothers herd the family flocks. Listen to him boast of his dreams: "You will bow down to me!"

See the brothers strip Joseph of his pride, his royal robe, and toss him in a pit.

Now let us think of another King. One who willingly set aside his royalty to be born in a stable.

And wonder . . .

We see a glimmer of God's plan right here in Joseph's robe.

If the Author of Scripture can whisper his plan across generations with a simple robe, how much more can we trust his authorship in our own lives?

Today is the Feast of the Immaculate Conception. See page 39.

Celebration!

(Families)

Focus Passage: *(Read aloud)* Genesis 37:3–4; 50:20

Now Israel loved Joseph more than any other of his sons, because he was the son of his old age. And he made him a robe of many colors. But when his brothers saw that their father loved him more than all his brothers, they hated him and could not speak peacefully to him.

[Joseph said to his brothers,] "As for you, you meant evil against me, but God meant it for good, to bring it about that many people should be kept alive, as they are today."

Jesse Tree Symbol & Description: Do you ever ask "why"? Joseph might have asked "why" many times. Why did his brothers take his coat? Why did they send him away to Egypt? Why did he spend years in prison? He was innocent! Joseph didn't know that God had a much bigger plan. God needed Joseph to be in Egypt so that Joseph could help many other people. God can use anything in our lives for his good purpose.

Today's Song: *Adam Lay Ybounden* dates back to around the year 1400 and may be the work of a wandering minstrel. Consider the *felix culpa,* or blessed fault, discussed by St. Thomas Aquinas as he described the beauty and joy necessitated by the Fall. Not the least of these graces are the Virgin Mary's example of faithfulness, and Christ's sacrifice. As Joseph understood, what was intended for evil, God turned to glory!

Family Reflection: It was a magnificent gift, this coat fit for a king. An honor Joseph even dreamed—yes, he dreamed of his ten older brothers bowing down to him.

Did he regret talking about this dream when his brothers' envy almost turned to murder?

They ripped his royal coat off his back and sold him.

As Joseph trudged beside other slaves, bound and hungry, he may have wondered what his dream meant now. And he wondered again when he spent long years in prison in a faraway land. All this suffering because of a coat and a dream.

Joseph knew of God's promise, that Abraham was given a blessing that passed to his father, Jacob. All the peoples of the earth would be blessed through them. Wouldn't they?

The whole land—Egypt and the countries beyond—was in desperate need. They'd had years of no rain and no grain. The people faced starvation and death.

By now Joseph was no longer a slave or a prisoner. He had been rewarded and blessed, and he was a ruler in his faraway land.

He could save his brothers, the very ones who wanted to kill him, and so many others. Through Joseph came an end to hunger; through him came blessing.

All because of a coat and a dream.

Together Time: *(Discuss the following questions)*

- What gift did Jacob (renamed Israel) give his son Joseph? Why was it special? *(Answers will vary from the coat's beauty to its significance.)*
- How was the promise to Abraham and Jacob continued in Joseph's life? How is Joseph like Jesus? *(They were blessed to be a blessing, and through Joseph many, even people outside Joseph's family, were saved from starvation, just as Jesus's sacrifice offers salvation to those outside the people of Israel.)*
- Have you ever experienced an "evil" that God used for the good of you or others?

PRAYER

O God, who gives us a gift by his grace:
that we should be made righteous instead of ungodly,
and blessed instead of miserable:
Help us to appreciate your gifts
and to persevere through all circumstances,
through Jesus Christ our Lord.
Amen.

—*Adapted from* Ancient Collects,
William Bright, 1902

CELEBRATE

THE FEAST OF THE IMMACULATE CONCEPTION

The angel Gabriel greeted Mary with the words, "Hail, full of grace!" (Lk. 1:28, NCB). What did he mean, *full of grace*?

Years earlier, a faithful young woman named Anne had heard God's whisper telling her to marry, not one of her handsome young suitors, but a plain but godly man named Joachim. Anne considered the qualities of the heart above beauty.

The couple married, but month followed month, year followed year, and still Anne did not conceive a child. The faithful couple gave generously to the temple, prayed fervently, yet remained childless.

According to some ancient traditions, Joachim sought prayer at the temple. He was harshly scolded and told that his childlessness was a sign of God's rejection. In shame and sorrow, Joachim hid himself among the shepherds of the land.

While in his self-imposed exile, Joachim met an angel who instructed him to find Anne at the city gate, promising that they would have a highly favored child.

Anne, aching in heart because of her husband's long absence, also received this news and rushed to the gate to meet her husband.

As promised, they soon conceived a daughter, Mary, whom they would dedicate to God's service. God's purpose was far greater than Anne and Joachim could have imagined. Their daughter would be the dwelling place and mother of God!

Like Eve, Mary was brought into this world without sin. Eve had no sin because she was created perfect, only later disobeying and bringing sin into the world. God chose Mary at her conception to one day carry Jesus in her womb. From her would be born the reversal of Eve's curse!

And so, God did the same for the second Eve as he had for the first—made her immaculate, spotless.

Mary, at the moment of the angel Gabriel's greeting, had a choice like Eve's. She could accept God's purpose for her in obedience or she could go her own way. Around the year 180, St. Irenaeus wrote, "The knot of Eve's disobedience was untied by Mary's obedience: what the virgin Eve bound through her disbelief, Mary loosened by her faith" (St. Irenaeus of Lyons, *Against Heresies*, Bk. 3, Chap. 22).

And so, the spotless virgin became the very first to eat from the tree of life as she carried the fruit of that tree within her womb.

Make Moravian Spritz

Moravian Spritz are Czech spiced cookies fragrant with cinnamon, clove, and ginger. As the aroma of these cookies fills your home, reflect on how Mary was said to have a sweetness and fragrance like the spice-filled anointing oil used in the temple. "Like cinnamon and fragrant cane, like precious myrrh I gave forth perfume; Like galbanum and onycha and mastic, like the odor of incense in the holy tent" (Sirach 24:15, NABRE). Consider mixing the dough up to ten days ahead to allow the spices to mingle—and to train your patience.

Moravian Spritz Recipe:

1 cup molasses
1/2 cup butter or shortening, softened
1 cup brown sugar
1 tablespoon red wine (sub: grape juice or white vinegar)
1/2 tablespoon baking soda
3 1/2–4 cups all-purpose flour or 1:1 all-purpose gluten-free flour
1 teaspoon ginger
2 teaspoons cinnamon
2 teaspoons cloves
1/4 teaspoon salt
optional: a pinch each of nutmeg and allspice

To Do:

- Cream butter, sugar, and molasses. Add wine, grape juice, or vinegar and mix thoroughly.
- In a separate bowl, combine spices, salt, soda, and 3 cups flour, and whisk together.
- Add dry mix to the butter mix, adding more flour until a very stiff dough is formed. The dough will be very stiff but should be soft enough to press into a ball.
- Chill for one hour or until firm (alternately, allow to rest in the refrigerator for up to ten days). Roll onto a well-floured surface and cut with cookie cutters.
- Bake at 275° for 8–10 minutes. Cookies should be crisp when cool.
- Gluten-Free tips: Mix for an extra several minutes. Roll dough between floured parchment paper or plastic food wrap to prevent sticking. Transfer to a baking sheet with a wide spatula. Baking time may need to increase slightly.

Tiny Tot Tip: Purchase or make a batch of cinnamon spice play dough. Let your toddler roll and cut their own cookies with cookie cutters. For an easy play dough recipe visit the Joy of Advent website. You'll find other celebration ideas here, too.

DECEMBER 9

MIRIAM AND A BASKET IN THE REEDS

Prepare Your Heart

(Teens & Adults)

Scripture: Exodus 2:1–10

Personal Reflection: Miriam was a child of Yes born into a world of *No*.

No, said Pharaoh to the ever-multiplying Hebrews, and he commanded that their sons be thrown into the Nile. *Yes,* said Miriam and her mother to Moses's life, even at the risk of their own. Imagine Miriam peering between the reeds. Imagine her trembling legs as she presented herself to the Egyptian princess.

Are we children of *Yes* in our world of *No*?

The world says *No* to purity—so old-fashioned and outdated, it says. The world says *No* to selflessness—do what makes ME happy, it says. The world says *No* to God—belief in the unprovable, the unseen, is absurd, it cries.

Reflect this season on how we might say *Yes* to God and *No* to the distractions, darkness, and deceptions of the world.

Jewish tradition credits Miriam's courage and faith for the people's exodus from Egypt. It was she who watched over Moses and ensured his life so he might lead the people to freedom. And according to tradition, a well of water followed Miriam as she and the people wandered in the desert, sustaining them.

The Jewish teaching continues that the *future final redemption of the whole world will come through the merit of one righteous woman.*

We might think of another young woman . . . a young woman, blameless in the sight of God, who also said *Yes*, even when culture, tradition, and reason would have her say *No*.

It was this righteous young woman who kissed the infant cheek of the true Final Redemption.

Celebration!

(Families)

Focus Passage: *(Read aloud)* Exodus 2:3–4

When she could hide him no longer, she took for him a basket made of bulrushes and daubed it with bitumen and pitch. She put the child in it and placed it among the reeds by the river bank. And his sister stood at a distance to know what would be done to him.

Jesse Tree Symbol & Description: Do you remember another story about a boat that saved people from a flood? It's hard to imagine Moses's tiny basket as an ark like Noah's, isn't it? But in the Bible, the same word is used for both. Moses's big sister didn't know if the tiny ark that held her baby brother would save him. Maybe it would leak. Maybe crocodiles or other wild animals along the Nile would find him. Miriam surely didn't think her brother, born to a Hebrew slave, would be raised as a prince! Jesus was laid in a manger as a tiny baby, and he is God's Son. Do you ever wonder if Mary knew who her son would be?

Today's Song: *Mary, Did You Know?* was written by Mark Lowry in 1984 and first released in 1991. Consider how little Miriam knew as she followed that basket through the reeds—her brother's very survival was in question, and she certainly never imagined he would grow up to foreshadow Christ and save a nation.

Family Reflection: *Surely, God is watching!* Miriam may have thought. *Surely, God has a plan for my brother's life!*

As Miriam watched the tiny basket with Moses inside, what did she fear? Perhaps crocodiles or leaks in her mother's handmade boat. Perhaps she feared for her life—what she was doing was illegal. Baby Moses was not supposed to live.

And yet he did; he floated away in a tiny boat made of reeds.

Many Bible translations use the word "basket" for Moses's small boat. Isn't it interesting that the Hebrew word used for Moses's boat of reeds is translated in another story as *ark*? Yes, the same *ark* as in Noah's story.

How could the same word be used for two very different boats? One was made of wood, the other of reeds.

One boat rescued Noah and his family from the waters of the flood, and Moses's tiny ark saved his life from the waters of the Nile.

Because of Noah's ark, humans continued to live on earth. Because of Moses, the people of Israel escaped slavery in Egypt and were set free.

Both ships—one enormous, one sized for a baby—were part of God's plan. Through each, God saved his people.

Together Time: *(Discuss the following questions)*

- Why did Miriam and her mother put baby Moses in a basket on the Nile? *(Pharaoh decreed that all baby boys would be thrown in the Nile, and they wanted to save Moses.)*
- How is Noah's ark like Moses's little "ark" basket?
- How do Moses and Noah foreshadow Jesus and his saving work? *(Both stories tell of how God works to save his people and are* types *or early shadows, like arrows, that point to Jesus.)*

PRAYER

In your unfailing love, O Lord,
you lead the people whom you have redeemed.
And by your invincible strength
you will guide them to your holy dwelling.
You will bring them in and plant them, O Lord,
in the sanctuary which your hands have established.
Thank you, O Lord, for your unfailing provision.
Amen.

—Adapted from The Song of Moses, Exodus 15

DECEMBER 10

PASSOVER LAMB

Prepare Your Heart

(Teens & Adults)

Scripture: Exodus 11:1; 12:21–32 & Matthew 26:26–29

Personal Reflection: The people of Israel stood, belts fastened, sandals on, ready for travel as they ate the Passover feast. After generations of oppression, finally it was time. . . .

The reason for their flight seems obvious—freedom. But the reason Moses gave Pharaoh was not freedom, but rather God's words, "Let my people go, so that they may worship me" (Exod. 10:3b, NIV).

Moses asked for the Hebrews to leave to worship God, and when Pharaoh offered a partial exodus, Moses insisted on their livestock leaving as well because they needed "to have sacrifices and burnt offerings to present to the LORD our God" (Exod. 10:25, NIV).

A lamb slaughtered, one for each household, fully consumed, blood on every doorpost—that Passover meal would become a worship service.

The Israelites had no churches, no temples, no tabernacle. While praise, song, and prayer were often present, at the *center* of worship was sacrifice. That first hastily eaten meal of lamb and unleavened bread would become part of a worship service to be reenacted every year, a service still practiced in Jesus's day.

At the Last Supper, as Jesus reclined at table with his disciples, he did not follow the traditional Passover celebration. He broke the unleavened bread, and instead of pointing back to Moses who led the people out of Egypt, Jesus spoke of what lay ahead, to the new Lamb of sacrifice, to his own body and blood. We may all eat of the Passover Lamb, now and forever!

Might we offer back our bodies, here and now, as living sacrifices as our "spiritual act of worship" (Rom. 12:1, NCB)?

PRAYER

Christ, our Passover Lamb, has been sacrificed for us, therefore, let us keep the feast, not with old leaven, nor with leaven of vice and malice and wickedness, but with the unleavened bread of purity, nobility, honor, sincerity, and truth. Amen.

—Adapted from 1 Corinthians 5:7–8

DECEMBER 11

SPIES TO THE PROMISED LAND

Prepare Your Heart

(Teens & Adults)

Scripture: Joshua 2:1–21

Personal Reflection: Only five women are listed by name in Jesus's family tree. Tamar, who tricked her way out of the helplessness of being a childless widow; Bathsheba, whose husband was killed to cover King David's sin; Ruth, a desperate young widow from a foreign land, and Rahab. . . .

How did a prostitute find her way into Christ's lineage?

Some say Rahab was a woman of financial means achieved by illicit acts, others that she was coerced, sold, or humiliated into her position. However she arrived at her place in life, the true question is *why her*?

Only a breath after marching across the Red Sea's dry seabed, the people of Israel had already broken their promise. They had worshiped a golden calf. This nation, God's chosen people, would be unfaithful so often God would call *them* prostitutes.

Rahab was a prostitute but perhaps she is also a promise.

Faithless Israel has an opportunity in Rahab to be faithful, to live a new life. And since she is not of Israel's people, the blessing that will come into the world through her descendant is available to us all, because her story doesn't end when the wall of Jericho crumbles.

Generations later, an angel would visit another young woman, the fifth woman in Christ's lineage, with the most amazing news. A baby, born to a virgin. She was asked to believe the impossible. As Rahab answered the spies, "[a]ccording to your words, so be it," young Mary would say in faith, "let it be to me according to your word."

Celebration!

(Families)

Focus Passage: *(Read aloud)* Joshua 2:21

And she said, "According to your words, so be it." Then she sent them away, and they departed. And she tied the scarlet cord in the window.

Jesse Tree Symbol & Description:

What does it mean to have faith? Rahab lived in one of the strongest cities in the land. The city was famous because it had a strong wall. Everyone said the wall was impossible to break. They said the city of Jericho would stand forever. But when spies came, Rahab believed in the power of God. She believed in God more than she believed in her city. Rahab put a scarlet cord in her window. When Jericho's walls fell down, she was safe. Scarlet is a shade of red. In the Passover story, the Israelites who painted red blood on their doorposts were saved, just as Rahab was saved by putting a red cord in her window.

Today's Song: *O Holy Night* was written in French in 1843 by the poet Placide Cappeau to celebrate a church organ renovation and was adapted into English by John Sullivan Dwight in 1855. Picture Rahab blinking in the dawn of that "new and glorious morn," seeing how she was rescued from Jericho's total devastation.

Family Reflection: Imagine a window high in a stone wall. In the window hangs a cord, brilliant scarlet, swaying gently as spiderweb cracks form in Jericho's mighty walls.

It was said the walls of Jericho were unbreakable. Yet as Israel's trumpets blast, stones in this great, unbreakable wall begin to crumble, first one, then more, until whole sections collapse.

Miraculously, when the cloud of dust clears, one small section of wall remains, and in it a window, the scarlet cord blowing in a desert breeze.

As the army charged through the rubble, they were told to destroy everyone in the city (Josh. 6:17). They would pass over just one home, the one marked by a cord in the window, a cord the color of blood.

Who, of all the people in Jericho was saved?

Rahab, who hid Israelite spies, who lied to Jericho's king. Rahab, who believed in the true God of Israel more than in the great, unbreakable walls of Jericho.

Of all the people in Jericho, only Rahab and those in her house were saved because she believed. Rahab is another hint of God's plan. The promise to Abraham was not just for Israel, it was for the whole world. Including us!

Together Time: *(Discuss the following questions)*

- Who was Rahab and where did she live? *(She lived in Jericho, a powerful city that Israel was told to conquer.)*
- Is anything in Rahab's story similar to the Passover story? *(Answers will vary. Draw attention to the details: the Israelites painted red blood around their doorposts to save them from the Angel of Death, and Rahab hung a red cord in her window to save her family from death.)*
- Rahab was not an Israelite. Why is that important to us? *(Talk about the New Covenant that comes through Jesus's blood that is for the whole world.)*

PRAYER

Lord, be with us this day,
Within us to purify us;
Above us to draw us up;
Beneath us to sustain us;
Before us to lead us;
Behind us to restrain us;
Around us to protect us.

—St. Patrick,
Apostle of Ireland
(c. 389–461)

DECEMBER 12

HANNAH'S PRAYER

Prepare Your Heart

(Teens & Adults)

Scripture: 1 Samuel 1:9–18, 1:27–2:10 & Luke 1:46–55

Personal Reflection: We've seen a theme of favor this season: Jacob the unfavored son and Joseph the favorite. Hannah the favorite wife, but unfavored by God, or so it seems because her womb is closed, a fact her husband's other wife makes known with mockery and taunting at every turn.

We might notice a similarity between Hannah and Sarah, whose promised son came in her old age. Yet looking forward, we find an even more striking parallel—another faithful young woman who, like Hannah, would bear a son consecrated or given over to God's service.

Both Hannah and Mary sang songs of praise recorded in Scripture.

The same themes run through their songs, nearly parallel until the end. Hannah's song continues beyond Mary's with lines of prophecy. "He will give strength to his king and exalt the horn of his *mashiach* . . . anointed" (1 Sam. 2:10b).

But at the time of Hannah's visit to the temple, Israel does not have a king . . . yet.

Hannah is not in Jesus's family tree, but her son of promise would anoint the first two kings of Israel, including the greatest king, David, from whom would come Jesus.

Mary's song does not share Hannah's lines of prophecy, because it doesn't need to. Her son *is* the promised *mashiach*, the "anointed."

In Hannah's song, the unfavored find favor, God exalts the humble, feeds the hungry, upsets the world's expectations, and promises this woman with no king, a future King of Kings, the *mashiach,* Messiah.

Celebration!

(Families)

Focus Passage: *(Read aloud)* 1 Samuel 1:27–28a (NABRE)

"I prayed for this child, and the LORD granted my request. Now I, in turn, give him to the LORD; as long as he lives, he shall be dedicated to the LORD."

Jesse Tree Symbol & Description: Have you ever made a "pinkie promise"? Many consider a pinkie promise to be unbreakable, far more serious than an ordinary promise. Hannah made a pinkie promise with God. If he gave her a baby, she would give that baby back to him. It must have hurt Hannah's heart to let her only son live at the temple, far away from home. But she honored her promise, and God blessed her with five more children! God gave us his Son, Jesus, because he also made a promise—far greater than any pinkie promise! He promised he would bring us to him, to heal the brokenness introduced by Adam and Eve's sin.

Today's Song: *Bring a Torch, Jeanette Isabella* was originally a dance tune for the French nobility first appearing in 1688. The song tells the story of two farmhands who find baby Jesus. Isn't it interesting that both Hannah and Mary describe themselves as "handmaids" (1 Sam. 1:11; Lk. 1:38)?

Family Reflection: What is a "prayer of the heart"? The obvious answer is that it's a prayer not spoken aloud, rather said in thought, in the *heart.*

It is also a prayer that fills our whole heart.

It's a deep longing so big, so great . . . like Hannah's desire for a son. Hannah begged, *"give to your servant a son."* And then she promised, *"then I will give him to the Lord all the days of his life."*

God heard the prayer of Hannah's heart and gave her a son.

Surely God wouldn't expect Hannah to give preschool-aged Samuel back to the temple, would he?

The law of Israel didn't require Hannah to give her son to God—she could have given money instead.

But Hannah had promised.

More than promised, she had *vowed.*

We live in a world of contracts. We sign on the line, and if we change our minds, we hire a lawyer. A vow, a *covenant,* is not a contract. Strangers can enter into contracts with one another, but a covenant requires a relationship. It's a promise backed not by lawyers, but by love.

Hannah received the desire of her heart, and in obedience, she gave him back to God.

God's promise to Abraham was not *just* a promise, it was a covenant. God would also give his very own Son . . . to us, to bless the whole world.

Together Time: *(Discuss the following questions)*

- What was Hannah praying for? *(She was praying for a baby!)*
- Why did Hannah bring Samuel back to the temple? Would you have done the same?
- Have you ever made a solemn promise or vow to God? (*If you answer this prayer, I will . . .)* What did you do?

PRAYER

O Lord, plant in me the root of all blessings, the fear of you in my heart so I will be humble and obedient, meek and patient. O Lord, grant me to love you with all my mind and soul, and always to do your will. O Lord, protect me from certain people, and demons, and passions, and from every other harmful thing. O Lord, do your will in and through me, a sinner. Amen.

—Adapted from St. John Chrysostom (347–407)

DECEMBER 13

Whispers in the Night

Prepare Your Heart

(Teens & Adults)

Scripture: 1 Samuel 3:1–14, 19–20 & Luke 2:52

Personal Reflection: Those wretched sons of Eli, offending everyone, including God Almighty, with their wildness and wickedness.

As sons of the high priest, they should have been walking in their father's footsteps, yet Eli's ears tingled with reports of his sons' wickedness. Did Eli chastise them for the offense against God?

He recognized that they sinned against the Lord, but Eli's focus was on the report, on what people were saying, not on what his sons were doing.

The opinion of man was more important than the honor of God.

It is no surprise Eli's lectures went unheeded, nor that his sons "did not know the Lord" (1 Sam. 2:12).

We're told that Eli suffered from the physical blindness of age, but perhaps he suffered a spiritual blindness as well. His faith was wrapped up in rapport with the people, their respect and honor, and in the ritual of temple observances. God was one to appease, as Eli said, "If someone sins against the Lord, who can intercede for him" (1 Sam. 2:25)? To Eli, God was not someone to *know*. As a father, he could not lead his sons to a relationship with God when he had not traveled that path to God already himself.

Eli, in his blindness, couldn't hear the voice of God. But an untutored child such as Samuel could, and did. Through the child of faithfulness, of a vow unbroken, the Lord anointed Israel's greatest human king. And from this king would one day come another child of faithfulness, one who would not only hear God's voice but would *be* God's voice.

Every walk leaves footsteps, even Eli's. Perhaps his sons *did* follow in their father's footsteps, and the better question for all of us is, where do our footsteps lead?

Today is St. Lucy's Day! See page 63.

Celebration!

(Families)

Focus Passage: *(Read aloud)* 1 Samuel 3:10

And the Lord came and stood, calling as at other times, "Samuel! Samuel!" And Samuel said, "Speak, for your servant hears."

Jesse Tree Symbol & Description: Close your eyes and listen. What do you hear? You hear the sounds around you. You might even hear things you don't normally hear—the buzz of the lights overhead or your own breathing. Eli was a priest, so if anyone heard God's voice, it *should* have been he. But he didn't hear God's voice. Late at night Samuel heard God. And Samuel obeyed. Are we listening for God? Will we obey his voice?

Today's Song: *Still, Still, Still* is an Austrian folk tune first appearing in print in 1865. Imagine Samuel in the still of night, the light of the Lamp of God keeping vigil, hearing the voice of God.

Family Reflection: Imagine young Samuel curled on the temple floor, blinking in the glow of the Lamp of God. Had someone called his name?

The lamp lit the space, golden light gleaming on the curved branches, each one like a tree branch topped with an almond flower.

Did Samuel yet know what the lamp meant?

This tree-shaped lamp reminded the people of God's power to give life, of Adam and Eve's sin, and of their future hope.

Someday God would save them.

Someday they would eat from the Tree of Life!

Imagine Samuel rubbing sleep from his eyes, gazing at the lamp.

Samuel! Samuel!

The voice wasn't Eli's. It was God's, the call so quiet it didn't wake Eli or any of the others who served in the temple.

God's voice does not come in brilliant, flashing lights, but in a flame. A single flame is tiny, but it is bright enough to light the way.

In the glow from the Lamp of God, Samuel answered the voice: "Speak, for your servant hears."

Many years later God's voice came again . . . in the stillness of a stable.

Again, God's voice was not the great shout of a King. No, his voice was as thin and fragile as a newborn baby's cry.

Together Time: *(Discuss the following questions)*

- What did Samuel hear? *(The Lord calling his name.)*
- Jesus is called the Light of the World. How might that name relate to Samuel's story? *(Answers will vary. Draw attention to the Lamp of God and how it represented God's promise to make a "new Eden," and how God accomplished this promise through Jesus.)*
- Reflect on a time when you heard God's whisper. If you heard it, did you heed it?

PRAYER

O Lord my God, say to my soul, I am your salvation. Say it so that I can hear it. My heart is listening, Lord; open the ears of my heart and say to my soul, I am your salvation. Let me run toward this voice and seize hold of you. Amen.

—Adapted from St. Augustine (354–430)

CELEBRATE
ST. LUCY'S DAY

In the glow of candlelight on damp stones, Lucy's footsteps were nearly silent. The year was AD 304.

Lucy carried bread in one arm, blankets in another, the wreath of candles on her head lighting the way. People crept out from hiding places, eager for food, warmth, news. A great persecution had swept the land: all Christians were wanted criminals, their punishment exile or death.

Early in her life, Lucy longed to give herself to God. She was young, beautiful, rich, and especially rich in her heart because of her love for Jesus. She ached for the poor and vowed to live her life serving the Lord and his people.

Her mother disagreed. Eutychia, a widow and seriously ill, worried for her daughter's future. So, she promised the beautiful young Lucy in marriage to a wealthy pagan man.

But how quickly a heart can change when it witnesses the power of God!

Eutychia and Lucy traveled to the shrine of St. Agatha in Catania, where Lucy prayed for a cure for her mother's illness.

Her prayers were answered; her mother was healed!

With the full blessing of her mother, the riches for Lucy's dowry were given to Christians suffering from persecution.

Many were in hiding because the governor required all to worship Roman idols. The faithful faced hunger and fear, and, if discovered, death.

It was Lucy's joy to serve them!

Her fiancé, however, was not as pleased to learn his future riches were being given away. He reported her to Paschasius, the Governor of Syracuse, as a Christian.

Lucy was arrested. Paschasius argued, ordered, and threatened Lucy in his attempts to make her worship idols.

She refused.

"No more of your words!" he cried. "The executioner will silence you."

Lucy calmly replied, "God's servants will always have words, for Christ our Lord has said to them, 'You shall be brought before governors and kings; take no thought how or what to speak, for it shall be given to you, for it is not you that speak but the Holy Spirit that speaks in you.'" (Matt. 10:18–20).

Paschasius ordered her dragged away, but as if she had been weighted to the ground, the guards could not carry her. Not even a team of oxen could pull her from her spot. They then piled wood around her for burning, but neither would the wood ignite. Lucy spoke of peace for the Church even as she was run through by a sword. We celebrate St. Lucy's courage and faith on this day she was born into heaven!

O Antiphon Luminary Display

Luminaries are portable, decorative lamps usually lit by candles. Used to light walkways or for home decor, homemade luminaries will remind us of the candles that, according to legend, St. Lucy wore on her head, leaving both hands free to carry more gifts for the persecuted Christians.

Supplies:

- paper and printer (or paper and waterproof pens)
- 7 clear glass jars of desired sizes
- Mod Podge® (or school glue and water)
- wide paintbrush
- O Antiphons
- 7 small flameless candles, 1 for each jar
- optional extras: glitter, ribbon, paints, tissue paper

To Do:

- Print the O Antiphon Luminary sheet from joyofadvent.com or, using waterproof ink, write them onto paper.
- Cut or tear the quotes into strips, one quote per strip. Each jar will be decoupaged with one quote.
- If using glue, mix 50/50 with water, or use Mod Podge® to decoupage the strips to the outside of your jars. You may tear the strips to arrange the words however you like! Add more glue or Mod with a brush, gently smoothing creases and folds. If the paper tears, don't worry! Align torn edges and keep going. Try not to overwork.

- Optional: Sprinkle with glitter while still damp if desired, or decorate with paints and glitter once dry.
- Dry completely, tie a ribbon around the mouth of each jar (optional), and place a flameless votive inside. Display on a windowsill, mantle, or location of your choice.
- From December 17–23 we will be praying the O Antiphons (prayers using the names of Jesus—more information on December 17). Draw your family's attention to your display. Can younger children find that day's Antiphon?

Tiny Tot Tip: Allow your toddler to decorate a jar with paints, stickers, glitter, or other items. Prepare for some mess! Once it is dry, place a flameless candle inside and enjoy.

DECEMBER 14

THE FAITHFUL DAUGHTER

Prepare Your Heart

(Teens & Adults)

Scripture: Ruth 1:1–18; 3:1–5

Personal Reflection: We hear a musical refrain, a certain melody repeated that comforts us in its familiarity. And so it is with Scripture.

Do we recognize this song? Famine, gnawing hunger, a family relocated at the promise of bread. After long years and great sorrow, a return home.

Israel followed Joseph to Egypt, and the people remained for many long years. After great sorrow, they departed, were fed in the desert with manna—bread from heaven—and came to the land of promise.

And Naomi, after suffering gnawing hunger, traveled to Moab with her husband. Great was her sorrow when she lost husband and sons; so great she changed her name to Mara, *bitter*, and vowed to return home.

Home to Bethlehem. Its literal translation: *House of Bread.*

Did she find promise as Israel did?

Yes!

Ruth, the faithful foreigner, clings to her, taking all of Naomi, her stories, her people, her sorrows, even her God into her own heart.

Through Ruth and Boaz, Naomi and Ruth are redeemed from poverty and desolation. As Ruth clung to Naomi, she now cleaves to Boaz, her redeemer.

Ruth's story is a refrain, a melody we will hear again.

Notes of this melody play in another woman, her name sharing the same root as Naomi's chosen name, *Mara*. She will likewise bear the sorrow of loss, the loss of her only son.

The song plays on—this Son offers redemption from poverty and desolation.

Are there notes yet to play? We are foreigners, strangers in a land of desolation. To whom will we cling?

Celebration!

(Families)

Focus Passage: *(Read aloud)* Ruth 2:11–12

But Boaz answered her, "All that you have done for your mother-in-law since the death of your husband has been fully told to me, and how you left your father and mother and your native land and came to a people that you did not know before. The LORD repay you for what you have done, and a full reward be given you by the LORD, the God of Israel, under whose wings you have come to take refuge!"

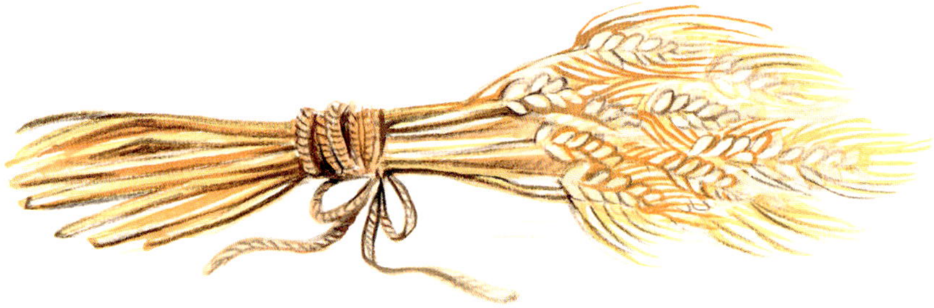

Jesse Tree Symbol & Description:

Imagine going to a different country: the language is different, the customs are different, even the food is not what you're used to eating. Now imagine going there and being poor and almost entirely alone. Ruth could have stayed in her own country. She could have returned to her parents' house as Orpah did, but Ruth loved Naomi so much that she didn't want her to be alone. Jesus will be with us the way Ruth was with Naomi.

Today's Song: *The Wayfaring Stranger* is an American folk song dating from the early 1800s and was at one point called the Libby Prison Hymn because a dying Union soldier wrote the lyrics on the wall of his cell in the notorious Confederate Libby Prison. Reflect on Ruth's hope as she journeyed through "this land of woe."

Family Reflection: Sweat beads on Ruth's forehead. She wipes it, aware of workers watching, and rests just a moment before returning to work.

Why did she follow Naomi so far from home, just to be a *gleaner*?

Jewish law required harvesters to leave dropped grain in the field rather than rake it up. The poor could glean, or gather what was left behind.

This dropped grain kept Ruth and Naomi alive.

When Ruth's husband died, she could have returned to her parents' home, but she had such deep love for Naomi that she would leave her homeland.

Yes, Ruth would trust Naomi's God, the God of Israel, even if she had to glean.

God provided food, and much more!

Someone watched Ruth glean: the owner of the land, Boaz.

Boaz heard of Ruth's faithfulness and married Ruth to become her *Kinsman Redeemer.*

A *kinsman* is a relative, someone in Naomi's extended family.

A *redeemer* is one who saves. Ruth would no longer be poor, living off the leftovers. She, with Boaz, was now owner of the field.

Through Ruth, God kept providing. He provided Israel with its greatest king. Ruth and Boaz were great-grandparents of King David. And from King David, many, many years later, God provided a Redeemer for us all, Jesus.

Together Time: *(Discuss the following questions)*

- Why did Ruth go with Naomi? *(Answers will vary. Draw attention to Ruth's love for Naomi and her people and God.)*
- How did Boaz help Ruth and Naomi? *(Boaz helped Ruth glean more grain, and ultimately he married her, providing security for her and Naomi.)*
- How is Ruth related to Jesus? *(She and Boaz are the great-grandparents of King David, and from David's line will come Jesus!)*

PRAYER

Lord, because you have made me, I owe you the whole of my love. Because you have redeemed me, I owe you the whole of myself. I owe you more than my whole self, but I have no more. Draw me to you, Lord, in the fullness of your love. I am wholly yours by creation; make me all yours, too, in love. Amen.

—Adapted from St. Anselm of Canterbury (1033–1109)

DECEMBER 15

ANOINTED SHEPHERD-KING

Prepare Your Heart

(Teens & Adults)

Scripture: 1 Samuel 16:1–13 & Acts 13:21–23

Personal Reflection: It's ordinary olive oil, the same we use in a heated pan or soothing lotion, and yet its use was far from ordinary. In ancient times, beyond its culinary and health uses (it's antiseptic!), olive oil was used to elevate everyday occurrences and items, consecrating or giving them fully to God.

Olive oil mixed with frankincense and other ingredients, in a recipe given to Moses, was used in the tabernacle. Anointing was used in worship and healing, but in David's day it specifically marked prophets, priests—especially the high priest, and, as with young David, kings.

Curiously, David was anointed not once, not twice, but three times for three different roles: prophet, priest, and king.

Samuel's anointing is followed with, "and the spirit of the Lord came mightily upon David from that day forward" (1 Sam. 16:13, NASB), initiating his prophetic role (Acts 2:29–30). David was also clearly King of Israel, but what about priest?

Not just anyone could serve as a high priest. When King Saul offered a sacrifice, he lost his rule, and Uzziah, a later king, was struck down with leprosy for attempting a priestly task. Yet David set up the Lord's tabernacle and offered sacrifices. The people were fed and David was blessed (2 Sam. 6:14–19).

The only other figure to unite the offices of Prophet, High Priest, and King is Christ himself.

Sit in wonder a moment—the intricate interweaving of the threads of God's plan: oil, anointing, consecration. Through David the shepherd boy, God pointed an arrow of providence directly to the coming Good Shepherd.

Celebration!

(Families)

Focus Passage: *(Read aloud)* 1 Samuel 16:7b & Acts 13:22b–23

For the LORD sees not as man sees: man looks on the outward appearance, but the LORD looks on the heart.

[H]e raised up David to be their king, of whom he testified and said, "I have found in David the son of Jesse a man after my heart, who will do all my will." Of this man's offspring God has brought to Israel a Savior, Jesus, as he promised.

Jesse Tree Symbol & Description: Think of the strongest, coolest superhero. Who did you pick? What if I told you the strongest superhero was actually . . . an elf named Bingo? There isn't really an elf named Bingo (probably), but the point is Samuel thought one of Jesse's older sons was sure to be God's Top Pick for King. They were tall and handsome. They looked like kings. But God knew that the little shepherd boy, Jesse's youngest son, was a "man after God's own heart" (see Acts 13:22). God chose a shepherd to be Israel's greatest king. God's Son, Jesus, is our King and the Good Shepherd.

Today's Song: *While Shepherds Watched Their Flocks By Night* first appeared in print in 1696 and is attributed to England's Poet Laureate Nahum Tate. Think of David as a shepherd boy, then ponder the fact that the Good Shepherd's birth would be announced first to shepherds in the very town of David.

Family Reflection: Oh, to be chosen as king! Incredible news! David must have started packing for his trip to the palace that same day.

Except, he didn't.

He returned to the fields and kept working as a shepherd. Later, he served Saul, the current king, as his cupbearer. David was chosen by God to be king, but he remained a "nobody." After David fought Goliath, Saul asked, "Whose son was that?" (see 1 Sam. 17:56). Saul had no idea who David was!

God's timing is not our timing. It would be at least *fifteen more years* before David was finally made king of Israel.

No one ever would have guessed, when David was a little boy out in the fields tending his father's sheep, that he would someday be the greatest king of Israel.

No one in David's day ever would have guessed that long after David's death, the kingdoms of Israel and Judah would fade to nothing and Israel would have no king at all. In that day, all would be awaiting one last King.

The angels sang the news to shepherds first, the news of Jesus, King of All, born that night in Bethlehem. The life of David, the shepherd-king, pointed toward Jesus, the Good Shepherd.

Together Time: *(Discuss the following questions)*

- Why did God pick David instead of Jesse's older sons?
- David was a shepherd. Why is that important as we think about Advent? *(God promised that another King would come from David, and Jesus was called the Good Shepherd.)*
- Can you think of a time when God surprised you or led you in a way you didn't expect?

PRAYER

Blessed Lord, give us your Holy Spirit to work in us daily. Give us true and lasting repentance, always willing to acknowledge our sins. Also keep us strong in our faith in the forgiveness of sins and in our purpose to amend our lives; through Jesus Christ our Lord. Amen.

—Adapted from Johann Gottfried Eichhorn (1752–1827)

DECEMBER 16

THREE DAYS IN THE GRAVE

Prepare Your Heart

(Teens & Adults)

Scripture: Jonah 3:10–4:11

Personal Reflection: Jonah the whiney prophet, the fearful prophet, the resentful prophet. Picture him on a ridge overlooking the city of Nineveh, burning in the desert sun, waiting for God to rain down fiery destruction on these, the worst enemies of Israel.

When God sees Nineveh's sorrow and their repentance and relents, picture Jonah stomping his feet and shaking his fists at God—because God showed mercy!

Yes, God's *mercy* so enrages Jonah that he begs for death.

We can only wonder at how unlikely Jonah is as a mirror of Christ. And yet he is. The parallels run deep: Jonah's self-sacrifice saves his shipmates, he spends three days in the grave of a fish's belly, and he's "resurrected" onto the shore. This parallel is confirmed by Jesus himself (Matt. 12:38–41).

Yet as Jonah pouts, the twisting, turning story takes on even deeper richness. We see a glimmer of Christ in a worm!

Wide, sheltering gourd leaves—representing the laws of Israel—spring up over Jonah, comforting him as he holds out hope for a cosmic light show of destruction. And when the *worm of God* withers the sheltering leaves of the law, Jonah is left defenseless against the relentless desert sun. Jonah is again irate. His expectations have been violated, his national pride offended. He wanted God to smite Israel's enemy!

Instead, God saved them.

One day soon a baby born in a stable, laid in a manger, would likewise turn law and expectation upside down and bring God's Light of grace into the whole dark world.

PRAYER

Come and show your people the way to salvation, O Lord, protect us in our weakness, and wash away our sins. Deliver us in your mercy from all evils, and grant us the height of good: through Jesus Christ our Lord. Amen.

—*Adapted from* Ancient Collects, *William Bright, 1902*

DECEMBER 17

IN THE YEAR THAT KING UZZIAH DIED

Prepare Your Heart

(Teens & Adults)

Scripture: 2 Kings 20:1–6, 8–19 & Isaiah 11:1

Personal Reflection: They're interesting things, tree stumps. As long as the soil is healthy, as long as there are roots, life continues. If nurtured, a new shoot can grow from something long considered lost.

The kingdom of Israel had long since split in two. One king reigned over ten Northern tribes, while another ruled in the South over two tribes called Judah and Benjamin. By the time of God's prophet Isaiah, the Northern kingdom had been in captivity for around 130 years.

If there were a pageant of Worst Kings of the Bible, Ahaz, Judah's current king, would be in the final lineup. Ahaz engaged in temple desecration and idol worship. He even created a cult and sacrificed his own children. Isaiah foretold that the line of Jesse—the kings of Judah including Ahaz—would be chopped down to a stump. But Isaiah also promised that a shoot would one day rise from that stump.

By the time of Mary's betrothal to Joseph, the kings of old were distant memories. Being in the line of David may have brought a certain prestige, as being a descendant of George Washington might give bragging rights to an American. But bragging rights brought no real privilege—it certainly didn't pay the bills.

Yet beneath the earth, in the belly of a woman, the first stirrings of the shoot from the stump of Jesse began to take hold. It rooted into her womb, grew a tendril of umbilicus as it drew life from humanity, and flourished in the rich soil of God's grace and Mary's willing heart.

Celebration!

(Families)

Focus Passage: *(Read aloud)* Isaiah 11:1–2

There shall come forth a shoot from the stump of Jesse,
and a branch from his roots shall bear fruit.
And the Spirit of the LORD shall rest upon him,
the Spirit of wisdom and understanding,
the Spirit of counsel and might,
the Spirit of knowledge and the fear of the LORD.

Jesse Tree Symbol & Description: Isaiah spoke about things that would someday happen. That's called prophecy. He warned kings to honor God and obey. But many of the kings did not honor God, and they did not obey. Kings were like trees: strong with wide branches that protected people. But so many kings were bad that God said he would chop them down. He promised that many years later, a new tree or king would grow from the old stump. That King is Jesus.

Today's Song: *O Come, O Come, Emmanuel* originated over 1,200 years ago as a monastic chant based on the O Antiphons, and ca. 1100 was developed into a Latin hymn. The most popular English translation, by John Mason Neale in 1861, includes the line, "O come, Thou Rod of Jesse." The original Latin Antiphons, chanted the seven days before Christmas Eve, form an acrostic in reverse. When the first letters of the antiphons are combined, they spell ERO CRAS. Translated, the words mean "Tomorrow, I will come."

Family Reflection: Can the hands of a clock go backward? Hezekiah asked for proof; he wanted the shadows on a sundial to move the opposite direction. And God did it!

King Hezekiah was so different from his father, Ahaz, and so like the great King David. Where King Ahaz built idols, Hezekiah tore them down. Where Ahaz sinned, Hezekiah obeyed.

When Hezekiah learned he would soon die, he begged for healing. God would reward such faithfulness and would give him fifteen more years to live. God would even prove his gift of healing with a miracle.

Hezekiah was so amazed by God's power and grace that when a prince of Babylon came to visit, Hezekiah couldn't help but tell him all about . . .

His riches.

His storehouses.

All his earthly treasures.

He said nothing about God's healing or his miracle. Not a single word.

Hezekiah's kingdom, grown tall as a tree, would be cut down. And after another seven kings, the tree with all its branches was felled altogether. The people of Israel would never have a king again.

Not until a young woman lay a precious baby in a manger. She was from David's line, David the son of Jesse. Jesus would grow like a tree from the stump of kings.

Together Time: *(Discuss the following questions)*

- How is a king like a tree? *(Answers will vary.)*
- Imagine you're Hezekiah. What's the first thing you would tell a visitor? What did Hezekiah actually do? *(He showed off his possessions without saying anything about the amazing miracle God had performed!)*
- A new tree can grow from a stump, as long as the roots and soil are healthy—how is your soil? In what are you rooted?

Beginning December 17 of each Advent season, and for the next seven days, a special antiphon (a short chant sung as a refrain) known as an O Antiphon is read. Each of the seven antiphons begins by addressing Jesus using an Old Testament title for the Messiah. Discover more about the O Antiphons at the Joy of Advent website.

PRAYER

O Wisdom, coming forth from the mouth of the Most High, reaching from one end to the other, mightily and sweetly ordering all things: Come and teach us the way of prudence. Amen.

—Translation of the Latin,
a medieval adaptation of Isaiah 11:2–3, 28:29

DECEMBER 18

DRY BONES IN CAPTIVITY

Prepare Your Heart

(Teens & Adults)

Scripture: Ezekiel 37:1–10, 24–28

Personal Reflection: Hardly a Christmas story, this vision of clattering bones and rising dead!

Another prophet long before Ezekiel also had a story of bones.

Men were hurrying to bury a companion as a band of marauders fast approached. The prophet Elisha's grave lay nearby, so they tossed the body in it. Immediately the dead man "revived and stood on his feet" (2 Kgs. 13:20–21), the Hebrew words identical to the dry bones who "lived and stood on their feet" (Ezek. 37:10).

Where did this life-giving power come from?

There is no power in bones, but there is power in *ru'ah*, translated *breath* or *spirit*. The same *ru'ah* hovered over the waters before creation, was given as *breath* to Adam and Eve, refers to the Holy Spirit in Isaiah (63:11), and is used in the book of Ezekiel 51 times!

Elisha asked for a double portion of the spirit of Elijah, his *ru'ah,* and from there came the power even in his bones. Elisha's story ripples forward from the Kingdom of Israel, who, by Ezekiel's day, had long been in captivity. As Ezekiel stood among bones, Judah was now also in exile.

The people of Judah may have felt hopeless, and we may face hopelessness in this world. We are surrounded by spiritual death, lifelessness, and darkness.

But here God raised an army from bones! Where is our power for the battle ahead?

As the prophet Zechariah wrote, our hope comes, "Not by might, nor by power, but by my Spirit, says the Lord of hosts" (4:6).

Celebration!

(Families)

Focus Passage: *(Read aloud)* Ezekiel 37:24

My servant David shall be king over them, and they shall all have one shepherd.

Jesse Tree Symbol & Description: Do you ever think about how amazing your body is? God gave you bones and muscles and skin. But what we're made of is only part of what makes us alive. We have a spirit and a soul too. In our story about Ezekiel, God covers bones with flesh and skin, but those bodies aren't alive until God breathes life into them. He breathes life into each of us.

Today's Song: *The Cherry-Tree Carol* may have begun as a story written around 650, that then became a ballad sung as early as the fifteenth century. The vivid and imaginative imagery of a cherry tree bending in obedience to offer pregnant Mary fruit recalls the power of God over the natural and supernatural—dry bones made alive, and a kneeling cherry tree.

Family Reflection: The ancient Israelites buried their dead. Always (Deut. 28:26). A body left out in the open was dishonored, cursed.

Bones were not rare in Ezekiel's time. If people traveled, they might see piles of bones from long-ago battles. Armies often left the bodies of their enemies unburied, in a pile. Only bodies of enemies or those cursed would be left to become bones.

Imagine Ezekiel's vision: a valley of bones long unburied. No human could put bones back together and make them live. But as the angel said to Sarah and to Mary, nothing is impossible for God (Gen. 18:14; Lk. 1:37).

And so the cursed bones rattled. They joined together and put on muscles and skin, and they lived.

What a comfort the vision must have been. The great kingdom of Judah was like a tree chopped down, now nothing but a stump. Ezekiel's vision was a promise. The Holy Spirit will bring life, and from David the shepherd king will come a new Shepherd.

Jesus will reverse the curse of death, will raise us all, and will dwell with us forever. We truly serve a God for whom nothing is impossible!

Together Time: *(Discuss the following questions)*

- What happened to the dry bones in Ezekiel's vision? *(They were covered with flesh and skin and filled with the breath of life from God.)*
- How does Ezekiel's vision relate to us? *(We all suffer from spiritual death and are under the curse of death because of sin. Jesus will be the King who gives us full and eternal life.)*
- Have you ever seen God do what you thought was impossible? *(If needed, talk about miracles.)*

PRAYER

O Adonai, and leader of the House of Israel, who appeared to Moses in the fire of the burning bush and gave him the law on Sinai: Come and redeem us with an outstretched arm. Amen.

—Translation of the Latin,
a medieval adaptation of Isaiah 11:4–5; 33:22

Please see December 17 for more about the O Antiphons.

DECEMBER 19

JOSIAH'S DISCOVERY

Prepare Your Heart

(Teens & Adults)

Scripture: 2 Kings 22:1–2, 8, 11; 23:21–25

Personal Reflection: The kingdom had been dark for so long, so very long. In the temple, statues of Baal knocked against the Lamp of God, while in its gentle glow, women wove cloths used in idol worship. The most recent king was so wicked, his own people assassinated him. His eight-year-old son, Josiah, then took the throne.

Josiah had no visions, no dreams. He had no prophecies, and we're told of no stirring of the Spirit of God. And yet early in his reign, he changed everything.

Josiah's story is surprisingly well suited for the season of Advent.

Advent, from the Latin for *coming* or *arrival*, is a season first mentioned in the 400s as a time of preparation, of solemnity and alertness. We await the coming not just of Jesus, God incarnate, but his eventual return in glory and the final judgment of our world. It was not a time of parties and celebration, but rather a season of penance, contemplation, fasting.

Through Huldah the prophetess, Josiah heard the voice of God, and he believed and obeyed, remaining steadfast. He "did not turn aside to the right or to the left" from the way of King David (2 Kgs. 22:2).

We are all like Josiah. Few of us receive visions, few have prophetic dreams. Yet we all have access to the Teacher written of in Isaiah, "And when you turn to the right or when you turn to the left, your ears shall hear a word behind you, saying, 'This is the way; walk in it'" (Isa. 30:21 NRSVue).

Celebration!

(Families)

Focus Passage: *(Read aloud)* 2 Kings 23:25

Before him there was no king like him, who turned to the LORD with all his heart and with all his soul and with all his might, according to all the Law of Moses, nor did any like him arise after him.

Jesse Tree Symbol & Description: If you could be king or queen for the day, what would you do? Josiah was just eight years old when he became king. His father and grandfather before him were evil kings, but Josiah was good. He ordered God's temple to be repaired, and while repairing it, they found a book of the law. King Josiah was amazed and frightened—they weren't obeying God's laws! God's laws had been forgotten. Josiah cleaned out all the false gods from his nation because he wanted to follow the law of God.

Today's Song: *Silent Night* was written by Joseph Mohr in 1816 and first performed two years later at a Christmas Eve Mass in Austria. In Josiah's day, the light of hope had faded. Imagine the contrast between Josiah's horrifying discovery of laws long broken and Jesus's peaceful birth, redemption having now arrived.

Family Reflection: His running footsteps echoed through the palace halls, the high priest eager to show the king this new, magnificent find. A book! The law of God!

The young king listened carefully, then rose and tore his robes.

All in the palace went home that evening unsettled. A wind was blowing, change coming.

In the same temple where Samuel heard God's call, idols of false gods sat blindly. Yet people worshiped these idols. They had broken God's law, and God promised punishment.

Josiah started a deep-clean in Judah like no one had done before. He tore down idols, beat statues into dust, then took the dust outside Judah to cursed places. He went to tombs of wicked kings, removed their bones and burned them so far away not even the smoke or ashes would pollute the land.

He followed God's law with "all his heart and with all his soul and with all his might" (2 Kgs. 23:25). He celebrated Passover like it had never been celebrated before.

Although God waited until after Josiah's death, his kingdom still fell. The goodness of one man, even a king, could not repair the broken relationship caused by the Israelites' wickedness.

Only God could bring healing, and only by sacrificing a perfect Lamb.

Together Time: *(Discuss the following questions)*

- What did the high priest show to Josiah? *(The book of the law, likely Deuteronomy.)*
- Why did Josiah clean away all the idols? *(He wanted to purify the land, but no matter how pure we try to be, we cannot earn our way to God.)*
- As we await Jesus's birth, how are we making our hearts ready?

PRAYER

O Root of Jesse, standing as a sign among the peoples; before you kings will shut their mouths, to you the nations will make their prayer: Come and deliver us, and delay no longer. Amen.

—Translation of the Latin,
a medieval adaptation of Isaiah 11:1, 10

Please see December 17 for more about the O Antiphons.

DECEMBER 20

DANIEL'S FIRST TEST

Prepare Your Heart

(Teens & Adults)

Scripture: Daniel 1:1–16

Personal Reflection: We may have read about the *Daniel Diet*, a weight-loss fad touted as *the* model for right eating. It's true, God made vegetables good to eat, but what if the reason behind Daniel's food choices weren't related to the menu?

Daniel and his friends had been taken as children from the Jewish royal palace and the homes of Israel's wealthiest nobles. They would be educated by Babylon's wisest magicians and astrologers—those practicing divination and worshiping idols, activities not just forbidden but detestable to God.

And so from the very first day, before anyone had been offered so much as a snack, Daniel and his friends set themselves apart. They weren't in Babylon to make friends. They were in exile.

After ten days of testing, they didn't think, *We made our point, let's get the good eats!* No, they permanently took on their sparse diet. They remained in exile in their hearts with a physical, daily reminder.

And the difference showed, not just in their courage when facing fire or lions. The king himself said about Daniel, "I know that the spirit of the holy gods is in you" (Dan. 4:9, NIV).

We are also in exile, living in a world that honors idols—personal happiness, security, approval of others—instead of God. As we continue through Advent, we might search our hearts and ask, are we different from the world or are we dining at the King's table?

PRAYER

O Key of David and scepter of the House of Israel; you open and no one can shut; you shut and no one can open: Come and lead the prisoners from the prison house, those who dwell in darkness and the shadow of death. Amen.

—Translation of the Latin,
a medieval adaptation of Isaiah 9:6; 22:22

Please see December 17 for more about the O Antiphons.

DECEMBER 21

A GIRL NAMED ESTHER

Prepare Your Heart

(Teens & Adults)

Scripture: Esther 3:13; 4:12–17; 8:5–8

Personal Reflection: "Let your yes be your yes, and your no be your no." It's common advice, even if difficult to follow. The difficulty was known even in Esther's day, for it was engrained in Persian law. Once the king signed Haman's edict of destruction against the Jews, it was irrevocable.

The king's decree could not be revoked, but a new decree could be written. And such was Esther's task.

Like a stone tossed in a pond, events of the past ripple outward, gathering and colliding with other events to grow their meaning and significance. We've seen these ripples of meaning many times. In an early ripple, we saw another irrevocable edict given to Eve, one of separation from God and death for all generations. According to Jewish tradition, Esther is a new Eve, the fast she instituted reversing Eve's bite of fruit.

And yet the ripple continues beyond Esther, across hundreds of years to a small town of Nazareth. There, a young woman of such beauty, such obedience, such unsurpassable purity is so favored that the King of Heaven and Earth chooses her to be the mother of his Son.

Through Mary, a new decree was written, signed, and delivered to the people, wrapped in swaddling clothes and laid in a manger by the arms of a queen (Rev. 12:1).

Esther's name in Persian means Morning Star. Queen Esther was elevated in her exile to bring about her nation's deliverance under secular rule. Let us reflect on our own exile as we pray today, *O Oriens, O Morning Star, come and enlighten those who dwell in darkness and the shadow of death.*

Celebration!

(Families)

Focus Passage: *(Read aloud)* Esther 4:14b

"And who knows whether you have not come to the kingdom for such a time as this?"

Jesse Tree Symbol & Description: Have you ever been afraid? Queen Esther must have been terrified to approach the king without being invited. If the king didn't welcome her with his scepter, she would be executed. Esther didn't carry a sword or fight in any battles. Yet her courage saved her people. She obeyed and used the gifts God had given her. God had a purpose for her life and for her people. Without Esther, no one in Jesus's family tree may have survived! How can we discover God's purpose for our lives?

Today's Song: *Carol of the Bells*, originally a Ukrainian song composed in 1914, was adapted into an English Christmas carol by Peter J. Wilhousky in 1922. The intensity of the repetitions brings to mind the fervency of Esther's prayers as she prepared to enter the king's throne room, as well as the exuberant joy of the people when they learned of Esther's success.

Family Reflection: When Mordecai asked Esther, "Who knows whether you have not come to the kingdom for such a time as this?" he was talking about God's hidden providence.

Providence means God's care *in advance*, or God providing what is needed at just the right time. We saw God's providence in Joseph's life when he was taken to Egypt, and in Moses's when the Pharaoh's daughter adopted him. God's purpose, his providence, was at first hidden.

Esther's name in Hebrew, *Hadassah*, is related to the word for "hidden."

God's purpose is often hidden, but in Esther, God himself is hidden! God's name is never mentioned in the earliest Hebrew scrolls. Jewish people still celebrate a holiday called Purim. As part of their celebration, they read the book of Esther from start to finish. In that entire reading, God's name is not mentioned once.

Even unnamed, God is still working, always.

Throughout Esther's story and ours, God is working. He answers prayers, brings things to our hearts and minds, and directs our lives whether we're aware of him or not.

The most hidden providence of all time happened more than two thousand years ago. A baby, born in a stable, was God in human form.

Together Time: *(Discuss the following questions)*

- Who was Esther and what did she do? *(Answers will vary. Direct conversation to how she saved the Hebrew people through her courage.)*
- Does Esther's story remind you of any other stories in the Bible? *(If needed, draw comparisons to Joseph and Moses and even the Nativity story. Explore the many layers of symbolism in Esther's story.)*
- Talk about "hidden providences" you may now see in your own life.

PRAYER

O Morning Star, splendor of light eternal and sun of righteousness: Come and enlighten those who dwell in darkness and the shadow of death. Amen.

—Translation of the Latin,
a medieval adaptation of Isaiah 9:2

Please see December 17 for more about the O Antiphons.

DECEMBER 22

NEWS! NEWS!

Prepare Your Heart

(Teens & Adults)

Scripture: Luke 1:5–25

Personal Reflection: If we stretch our minds back to two earlier days of this busy month, we'll remember Sarah and Hannah. Both women longed for a child. Perhaps Zechariah of the New Testament thought of Sarah and Hannah as he prayed fervently, petitioning the Lord to fill his wife's womb. Years passed, and Zechariah's wife, Elizabeth, aged.

Had Zechariah given up praying by the time Gabriel met him in the temple?

It likely wasn't every day that an angel appeared to him in the temple. And he knew the story of Abraham and Sarah—as a priest, he knew all the Scriptures intimately. Plus, Gabriel's message was something *he had been praying for.*

But Zechariah's response wasn't joy, nor even wonder.

Instead he demanded, "How will I know?" His question was a challenge: *Prove it.*

So Gabriel proved it. He stated his name, his position, and repeated his message.

And then he provided a very strong and fitting sign in response to Zechariah's lack of faith—Gabriel struck Zechariah mute.

Do we ever pray without *really* expecting an answer? Have we ever asked for a sign from God? *Lord, show me which job offer to accept—give me a sign. Will I ever see an end to this illness? I need a sign.* Have we ever experienced a sign so powerful (or uncomfortable) that we couldn't possibly doubt the Messenger? Let us reflect on prayers that have been answered in our lives, even if (especially if!) they were answered in ways we did not expect.

Celebration!

(Families)

Focus Passage: *(Read aloud)* Luke 1:19–20 (NIV)

The angel said to him, "I am Gabriel. I stand in the presence of God, and I have been sent to speak to you and to tell you this good news. And now you will be silent and not able to speak until the day this happens, because you did not believe my words, which will come true at their appointed time."

Jesse Tree Symbol & Description: Have you ever seen an angel? Zechariah hadn't! We'd think Zechariah would believe whatever the angel Gabriel told him, wouldn't we? But Zechariah asked God's angel to *prove it*! The angel Gabriel did prove it—by making Zechariah unable to speak until the promised baby was born. If God "proved" his power like that, would we be convinced? A trumpet is today's symbol, which reminds us that Zechariah's baby, John, would have a very special announcement to make. He would have a powerful voice, which is the opposite of his father's having no voice at all.

Today's Song: *Joy to the World*, written in 1719 by Isaac Watts, was not meant to be a Christmas carol. Rather it interprets Psalm 98 and looks toward the second coming of Christ. How fitting a song as we reflect on the ministry of Zechariah and Elizabeth's son: to announce the Messiah and point the way toward Jesus.

Family Reflection: Zechariah and his wife had prayed for God to give them a baby. They had prayed all through their younger years. Now that they were old, did they still pray? They knew the story of Sarah, who had a baby of promise in her old age.

They knew God *could* give them a child.

Imagine Zechariah's joy when the angel Gabriel gave him the news. *You will finally be a father!* Except Zechariah did not react with joy. He asked the angel to prove it.

The angel took away Zechariah's ability to speak. He would be mute for months and months as a reminder that God keeps his promises.

But God may have had another reason for Zechariah's silence.

Zechariah's baby boy would have a very special mission. This child, John (called John the Baptist) would announce the coming of the Christ.

Zechariah's silence is the opposite of his son's mission of *announcing*.

This story tells us about the importance of words. Here Zechariah's words were taken away. Later, when Zechariah's son, John, was grown, John's words would be like a trumpet announcing the arrival of Jesus, who is called the Word.

Together Time: *(Discuss the following questions)*

- Why was Zechariah struck mute? *(His muteness was a sign of God's promise and a reprimand for his lack of faith.)*
- How might Zechariah's inability to speak relate to his son John's future ministry? *(John's ministry would involve announcing the coming Messiah, a strong contrast to Zechariah's silence.)*
- Share a time when you didn't expect God to answer your prayer or a time when God answered a prayer in a way you didn't expect.

PRAYER

O King of the nations, and their desire, the cornerstone making both one: Come and save the human race, which you fashioned from clay. Amen.

—Translation of the Latin,
a medieval adaptation of Isaiah 2:4; 9:7

Please see December 17 for more about the O Antiphons.

DECEMBER 23

MARY HAS A VISITOR

Prepare Your Heart

(Teens & Adults)

Scripture: Luke 1:26–45

Personal Reflection: Like Zechariah, Mary questioned the angel Gabriel's announcement, asking, "How can this be?"

Yet no admonition or muteness followed.

She had never "known a man," and she knew God would not ask her to break his own law to conceive a child. There was no reprimand from Gabriel because there was no doubt in her question—it was a question of logistics.

Plus, Mary knew well the laws of her day. Betrothal was a legally binding pre-marriage covenant. Any child conceived but not fathered by the betrothed would be proof of adultery, and the legal consequence for adultery was death.

Mary's faith appears to be as unshakable as Abraham's when he was told to sacrifice Isaac, because accepting Gabriel's message and agreeing to be Jesus's mother could have led to her death. Even if Joseph allowed her to live, she knew she could face the humiliation of being a single, unwed mother. Those who might prefigure her—Eve, Miriam, Hannah, Esther—cannot capture the humble simplicity and miraculous faith of the words, "Let it be to me according to your word."

Mary's cousin Elizabeth would later, when filled with the Holy Spirit, shout, "Blessed are you among women, and blessed is the fruit of your womb!" (Lk 1:42).

Envision the courage and faith of a young woman so willing to give her life over entirely to God that, as Mary herself said, "from now on all generations will call me blessed" (Lk. 1:48).

Celebration!

(Families)

Focus Passage: *(Read aloud)* Luke 1:38

And Mary said, "Behold, I am the servant of the Lord; let it be to me according to your word." And the angel departed from her.

Jesse Tree Symbol & Description: Has anyone ever asked you to do something impossible? The angel Gabriel told Mary that God wanted her to do the impossible. She would be mother to God's very own Son! She could have said, "Prove it," as Zechariah did. Instead, she had faith. She asked how she could possibly be a mother since she wasn't married, but when the angel explained, she said, "Let it be to me according to your word."

Today's Song: *Gabriel's Message*, first published in English in 1892, is based on a Latin folk carol developed in the Basque-speaking part of Spain and France, dating back to around the thirteenth century. This musical retelling of Gabriel's announcement to Mary reminds us how she will ever be called "Most highly favored Lady, Gloria!"

Family Reflection: Many stories in the Bible tell about God doing the impossible. God gives a child to someone who thought her womb was closed, such as Sarah, Hannah, and Elizabeth.

Each wanted a child.

Each had faith that God *could* provide, if only he would.

Mary had the same faith. Except she didn't ask for a child—not yet! She wasn't even married! Even so, God told her she would bear a very special child, Jesus, his Son.

For Hannah, Sarah, and Elizabeth, having a baby would be the greatest blessing of their lives.

For Mary, since she did not have a husband, having a baby now could be hard, or even mean her life was at risk.

Yet she still said "yes" to God.

Have we ever done something difficult? Perhaps we had to tell the truth about something we wanted to keep secret. Maybe we had to be kind to someone who had hurt us.

Let us all make Mary our model for every blessing as well as every trial. Let us all answer God as Mary did, "Let it be to me according to your word."

Together Time: *(Discuss the following questions)*

- What did Gabriel say to Mary? *(He told Mary she was highly favored and was chosen to be the mother of God's Son.)*
- How did Mary answer? *(While she asked a question, she faithfully and obediently offered herself fully to God's will.)*
- Have you ever faced an impossible request, obligation, or task that you believed was from God? How did you respond? What was the outcome?

PRAYER

O Emmanuel, our King and Lawgiver, the Expected of the Nations and their Savior, come to save us, O Lord our God. Amen.

—Translation of the Latin,
a medieval adaptation of Isaiah 7:14

Please see December 17 for more about the O Antiphons.

THE JOY OF CHRISTMAS

Celebration!

(Families)

Focus Passage: *(Read aloud)* Matthew 1:24–25

When Joseph woke from sleep, he did as the angel of the Lord commanded him: he took his wife, but knew her not until she had given birth to a son. And he called his name Jesus.

Jesse Tree Symbol & Description: Joseph surely wasn't happy to discover that his fiancée was going to have a baby! He may have been jealous, scared, sad, or deeply hurt. He could have embarrassed Mary, but he didn't want to hurt her, even though he may have felt hurt. Instead, he showed his love for Mary. Then, when an angel told Joseph in a dream to marry her anyway, Joseph believed God. He obeyed and became the earthly foster father to the Son of God. He would even teach Jesus to be a carpenter as he was.

Today's Song: *O Come, All Ye Faithful* may have been written in its original Latin, *Adeste Fideles,* as early as the thirteenth century, although the first text published was penned by John Francis Wade in 1751. This carol calls the faithful to worship, recalling a line from the Nicene Creed, "God from God, Light from Light." Traditionally it is the final anthem of the Midnight Mass at St. Peter's Basilica in the Vatican, and it leads us to do as the shepherds did and adore Christ the Lord.

Family Reflection: Through the season of Advent, we've been following shadows. So many stories in the Bible hold glimmers, like shadows, of things to come. Noah's boat saved humanity, blood on doorposts rescued the people from death, Jesus's blood offers salvation to all. In Joseph's story, we see another shadow.

Joseph and Mary were both in Abraham's family tree, both descended from King David. Jesus was born of Mary, but Joseph was his foster father and legal adoptive father. Jesus had as much right to the throne of King David as Joseph himself, even if he wasn't related to Joseph by blood.

God came to us in human form in Jesus for a purpose: to do what he promised. He told Abraham that all would be blessed through him. Glimmers in many stories have hinted at this blessing. Finally, the promise is fulfilled in Jesus.

The apostle Paul writes, "For you did not receive the spirit of bondage again to fear, but you received the Spirit of adoption by whom we cry out, 'Abba, Father'" (Rom. 8:15, NKJV).

As we think of Joseph's love for Mary and for her son, let us think too of God's love for each of us.

Through Jesus we are all adopted into God's family. We have the full rights to the inheritance of the King of the Universe!

Together Time: *(Discuss the following questions)*

- Do you think Joseph loved Mary? *(Answers will vary: Draw attention to Joseph's concern that Mary not be executed or shamed, and to his trust and obedience.)*
- Was Joseph Jesus's father? *(No . . . and yes. Joseph was not Jesus's biological father, but because he was married to Mary, he was Jesus's legal father.)*
- How would it feel to call God "Abba, Father" or "Daddy"?

PRAYER

Almighty God, who has given us his only Son, born of a virgin and taking on the nature of humanity, grant that we may be made new. As we are made your children by adoption and grace, renew us day by day through the Holy Spirit and our Lord Jesus Christ, who lives and reigns with you and the Spirit, ever one God, world without end. Amen.

—*Adapted from* Household Prayer,
P. G. Medd, 1864

CELEBRATE
CHRISTMAS EVE

Somewhere in the world right now, a child gazes up at Christmas tree lights, while another is shaking presents, crunching candy canes, or peering into their stocking.

Where did our favorite holiday symbols and traditions come from? We already saw how St. Nicholas's gift to the poor widower's daughters gave us the Christmas stocking. We'll soon see how the Christmas star reminds us of the star the Magi followed to find young Jesus. Where did other popular traditions come from?

Christmas Trees: Legends of the Christmas tree abound. Some claim Christians adopted the pagan tradition of bringing evergreens indoors during long winter months as a reminder that spring would return. Others credit St. Boniface, a seventh-century missionary and martyr who struck down the great Thunder Oak, symbol of the Norse god Thor's strength, in a single axe blow. It is said an evergreen grew from the stump, demonstrating Christ's power over false gods. Another likely origin is found in the medieval tradition of Mystery Plays performed as early as the 900s, in which the mysteries of the Old and New Testaments were acted out. At Christmas, a large evergreen Paradise Tree was the prop for the most popular play, the Paradise Play, the story of Adam and Eve's fall into sin. The Paradise Tree, dressed later with apples and small wafers representing Christ, eventually moved off the stage. The first Paradise Tree recorded was set up in a hospital at Freiburg, Germany, in 1419, and was decorated with apples, wafers, gingerbread, and tinsel. Popularity of the Paradise Tree spread. When laws in England pushed most outward signs of Christmas into private homes, the Paradise Tree remained, in the true spirit of an evergreen, quietly alive. It bloomed anew when, in the 1850s, Queen Victoria's German husband, Prince Albert, placed such a tree in the royal palace.

Lights: The earliest Christmas lights were candles used even in the early church to represent the Light of Christ. In older traditions, a large, white, decorated Christ Candle was lit on Christmas Eve and continued burning throughout Christmastide. In Germany, many smaller candles replaced the single candle and were arranged in displays such as in the Christmas Pyramid, topped with a star. During the sixteenth century, people in western Germany combined the Paradise Tree with Christmas Candles, and our modern glowing-with-lights Christmas tree was born.

Gifts: Today's gift-giving is said to represent the gifts of the Magi to Jesus. The tradition, however, may originate in a New Year's tradition of ancient Rome where people exchanged gifts of food and valuable items as tokens of good wishes for a happy new year. The custom gradually shifted from New Year's to Christmas, becoming tied to the gifts of the Magi and, in some countries, to St. Nicholas.

Carols by Candlelight

Christmas Carols of today often have roots in folksongs of the past. Many began as popular tunes with added Christian lyrics, others were initially Christmas poems, and some, like *O Come, O Come Emmanuel*, began centuries before in monasteries and churches. Have your own Carols by Candlelight celebration this evening, with or without a mug of traditional wassail.

Supplies:

- five to ten favorite Christmas carols
- paper and copier or printouts of the Carols by Candlelight Booklet from the Joy of Advent website
- candles and/or the luminaries created earlier this season
- optional: wassail, hot cocoa, and Christmas cookies

To Do:

- Print the Carols by Candlelight Booklet or write down the titles of your favorite carols.
- Light candles and dim the lights.
- Using accompaniment of your choice or lyric videos online, sing in celebration!
- Optional: Invite friends and consider walking your neighborhood, singing and praying blessings over the homes you pass.

Tiny Tot Tip: Toddlers love music! Provide your littles with instruments of choice (ones that won't drive you to distraction), and be sure to include *Away in a Manger* with the motions listed below.

Away in a manger
No crib for a bed
(Arms crossed in front to make a cradle)

The little Lord Jesus
Laid down His sweet head
(Cheek rested on praying hands as if sleeping)

The stars in the bright sky
Looked down where He lay
(Hands up, fingers moving like twinkling stars)

The little Lord Jesus
Asleep on the hay
(Cheek rested on praying hands again)

Find more Christmas Eve activities and resources at the Joy of Advent website.

DECEMBER 25, FIRST DAY OF CHRISTMAS

BEHOLD THE BABE!

Prepare Your Heart

(Teens & Adults)

Scripture: Luke 2:1–20

Personal Reflection: Oh, Little Town of Bethlehem! It's a place of wonder, of art and song, of joy and celebration.

True, Bethlehem was the birthplace of King David and was mentioned in prophecies of old (1 Sam. 16:18; Mic. 5:1; Matt. 2:6), but by Joseph's day, it was just a shepherd community. Why Bethlehem?

As a shepherd's community, it relates to two names of Jesus, Lamb of God and Good Shepherd. But the very word *Bethlehem* comes from the Hebrew word for house, *bayit*. Rather than a domestic home, this word implies a realm of authority—a founding ancestor, as in "the House of David." Bethlehem also stems from *laham*, meaning *to eat* or *bread*. Bethlehem is literally the House of God's Bread.

Bread was vital to Jewish life and to culture. Challah was served in weekly Shabbat or sabbath services, its covering of embroidered white cloth reminiscent of the dew on the manna God sent from heaven, and central in the Passover feast was the unleavened bread, broken by Jesus when he said, "This is my body, which is given for you" (Lk. 22:19).

Jesus, although born in Bethlehem, *came* from Nazareth. The root *Nazir* is a "consecrated one," *neser* is a precious green branch or shoot from a root, *nasar* involves keeping a promise or covenant. And so from the name of this town we might read: Christ, the consecrated one, keeps the promise of the shoot from the stump of Jesse!

Yes, this child born in House of Bread will become the new consecrated manna, the Bread of Life, a sheltering tree springing from ancient roots for the people throughout all ages.

Send your Twelfth Night Party invites! See page 185.

Celebration!

(Families)

Focus Passage: *(Read aloud)* Luke 2:10–12

And the angel said to them, "Fear not, for behold, I bring you good news of great joy that will be for all the people. For unto you is born this day in the city of David a Savior, who is Christ the Lord. And this will be a sign for you: you will find a baby wrapped in swaddling cloths and lying in a manger."

Jesse Tree Symbol & Description: Do we know the song *The Twelve Days of Christmas*? Today is the first day of Christmas. Today Jesus is born! Imagine being a shepherd. We're in the field, leaning on a staff. *One sheep, two sheep, three sheep*. Suddenly the sky fills with light and music. Angels! The shepherds heard the angels' message and found exactly what they said: a newborn baby sleeping in a wooden manger where animals kept their hay. Today is the beginning. It's the beginning of Jesus's life, the beginning of God's plan to save us, and the beginning of the season of Christmastide. For twelve days we will celebrate the joy of God's most important gift. He was born as a baby to be with us.

Today's Song: *I Saw Three Ships (Come Sailing In)* is an English folk carol, first printed in the 1600s, with today's lyrics appearing in a collection compiled by William Sandys in 1833. Traditionally, the birth of Jesus was said to have happened at midnight, so with dawn's first light, all the bells on earth would ring in Christmas Day's joyful announcement.

Family Reflection: Why would someone change their name? In the Bible, people's names were changed when their life or purpose changed.

Abram became Abraham when God promised he would become "father of a multitude of nations" (Gen. 17:4–5).

Naomi, happily married with two sons and daughters-in-law, became Mara, meaning *bitter*, after losing everyone but Ruth (Ruth 1:20).

The angel Gabriel announced Jesus's name before he was even conceived.

What does Jesus's name mean?

His name's meaning takes up far less space in the Hebrew dictionary than most other Bible people or places. *Yasha* and its various forms means *freedom* and *the Lord saves.*

Yet this tiny baby's name has amazing power. The Bible says the name of Jesus can save, can heal, can make evil flee!

And because Jesus is so full and overflowing, one name cannot contain all of who he is. There are more than one hundred other names for Jesus in the Bible. Here are just a few: Lamb of God, Good Shepherd, Bread of Life, Prince of Peace, Light of the World, King of Kings.

With the name of Jesus also comes a promise that every knee shall bend (Isa. 45:23; Phil. 2:10–11), beginning with the shepherds, who were first to greet the newborn King.

Together Time: *(Discuss the following questions)*

- Who were Jesus's first visitors? *(Shepherds, and how fitting because he is the Lamb of God and will be called the Good Shepherd!)*
- What does your name mean? Does it fit you?
- *Emmanuel* is a name of Jesus meaning *God with us.* How is God with you today?

PRAYER

Almighty God, give us grace that we may cast away the works of darkness, and put upon us the armor of light. Now in this mortal life when your Son, Jesus Christ, came to visit us in great humility, grant that in the Last Day, when Jesus shall come again, we may rise to the life immortal. Through Jesus, who lives and reigns with you and the Holy Spirit, now and ever. Amen.

—*Adapted from* Household Prayer, *P. G. Medd, 1864*

CELEBRATE
CHRISTMAS DAY

"You there," shouted the Lord Mayor of Canterbury. "Open your bakery at once!"

The baker stood in his shop's doorway. "But sir, 'tis Christmas."

Lord Mayor scowled. "By order of Parliament, business shall continue as on any other day."

A crowd had gathered on that London street in 1647 as the Lord Mayor strutted up and down, knocking on shop doors and ordering their owners to open for business. The celebration of Christmas had been outlawed.

The crowd shouted their disapproval. When the Lord Mayor continued knocking and ordering, someone in the crowd grabbed him by his suit lapel and shoved him into the gutter.

Soon the streets were overrun. Shouting and yelling filled the morning air, because the people of Canterbury wanted to keep their Christmas, whether Parliament allowed it or not. And so began what would be called the Plum Pudding Riots in favor of Christmas.

Despite the riots, the attack on Christmas would continue, and by 1652 Parliament would order, "No observance shall be had on the five-and-twentieth of December, commonly called Christmas Day." In much of England, any public display of Christmas, be it festivities, decorations, or worship services, resulted in fines or a few hours in jail. The people kept what they could of Christmas—family gatherings, food, festivities—in the privacy of their own homes.

Just eight years later, in 1660, the ban on Christmas was lifted, but Christmas had changed. Carols in praise of Christ's birth and its significance were being replaced by rollicking songs celebrating Figgy Pudding, and a general spirit of generosity toward the poor overshadowed the celebration of Christ at Christmas.

It seems our current culture loves Christmas just as much as those Plum Pudding rioters. Workers begin hanging lights and raising trees dressed in cheery red and green months in advance of the holiday. Christmas music takes over the radio waves as whole neighborhoods fill their lawns with signs of Christmas.

We may have already noticed something is still missing. Store displays feature Santa, reindeer, snowflakes, elves. Radio singers croon about sleigh bells, toy lands, crackling fires, and Christmas heartbreak.

Christ is scarcely part of Christmas.

And given Christ's absence, it's not surprising when, by tomorrow, most radio stations will be back to their regular lineup, and Christmas merchandise will be tossed into the mark-down bins as New Year's props take their place on store shelves.

Even so, today *is* Christmas.

Today is also the *beginning* of Christmas. It's the first day of Christmastide, the twelve-day *season* of Christmas.

As shops fling open their doors and the world moves away from celebration, let's *continue* to celebrate the mystery of Jesus, God incarnate, who gave us the greatest gift of all time—the sacrificial gift of himself.

The Christmas Pickle

The Christmas Pickle is widely thought to be a German tradition inspired by a story of St. Nicholas rescuing two schoolboys from a pickle barrel. Most modern Germans, however, aren't familiar with the tale or tradition. Others claim an American Civil War prisoner-of-war, malnourished and ill, asked his guards for a single pickle before he died. They complied, and that pickle gave him strength enough to survive and tell his story. What is known is that a glass-blowing company in Lausch, Germany, produced ornaments shaped as fruits and vegetables, including pickles, from as early as 1847. Once they learned of the myth, they began marketing their Christmas pickles, which quickly became their top seller. Most families allow the pickle-finder to open the first gift or to receive an extra gift. We allow that child to be "St. Nicholas" and pass out gifts one at a time to siblings, parents, and other relatives.

Supplies:

- a Christmas Pickle ornament

To Do:

- Before opening gifts, hang the Christmas pickle, careful to hide it deep in the tree, out of sight.
- The first child to find the pickle gets to pass out gifts to be opened, is the first to open their gift, or receives a small prize.

Tiny Tot Tip: Place a second (unbreakable) Christmas pickle ornament lower on the tree and encourage toddlers to find and re-hang it.

Who Is In Your Nativity?

Many families display at least one Nativity set, complete with all the characters of the Christmas story. Mary and Joseph with the manger take center stage, while shepherds, angels, animals, and the three Magi often fill in the scene. Nativity sets can enrich any generation's celebration of Christmas, inspiring us to imagine the scene in artful, beautiful ways.

Nativities can also be a teaching tool with a few small changes. First, when unpacking the display, set aside the baby Jesus figure (or the whole manger, if they are one piece) and keep it in a safe place. On Christmas Eve, place Jesus in the manger (or the manger in the scene), giving the whole family a visual reminder of the precious significance of the night.

The Magi, if your set includes them, can also be kept from the central scene. We display our Magi in a room far away from the Nativity, and over the twelve days of Christmas, gradually move them closer. On Epiphany, they complete their long journey and join the full Nativity scene. Why the long delay? Skip ahead to Celebrate Epiphany to find out (page 183)!

DECEMBER 26, SECOND DAY OF CHRISTMAS

HEROD, KING OF JERUSALEM?

Prepare Your Heart

(Teens & Adults)

Scripture: Matthew 2:1–4

Personal Reflection: Ah, the longing for a Messiah!

The people had been waiting so very long. As with their groaning in Egypt, they yearned again for the fulfillment of promise.

They were a people accustomed to waiting, but in this generation, their waiting had a new urgency, like a breath of spring sending life into a tree's buds. Scholars had pored over the prophecies of old, and some believed the coming of the Messiah, the return of King David, and a New Jerusalem were close at hand.

A few, such as the religious leaders, were not seeking a new king. "We have no king but Caesar" (Jn. 19:15), they would say, rather than relinquish the power given them by Rome. Others expected a strong military leader. Many, however, awaited a prophet and miracle worker who would demonstrate not man's power, but God's.

Apart from a select group of followers, no one considered Herod anything but a madman, despite the thirty years he spent calling himself King of the Jews.

Herod, infamous for his brutality and suffering a gangrenous infection in his groin so agonizing it drove him to attempt suicide and made him perpetually unclean by Jewish law, was most certainly *not* the Messiah, the anointed one, of the people's hope. Their new Moses.

Their new Moses, the true King of the Jews, now lay in a manger, and would soon repeat Moses's first miracle of water into blood (Exod. 7:20), except that Jesus would turn water into wine—his own blood (Jn. 2:1–11), and would part the gulf between heaven and earth to lead all people out of bondage.

Today is St. Stephen's Day. See page 129.

Celebration!

(Families)

Focus Passage: *(Read aloud)* Matthew 2:1

Now after Jesus was born in Bethlehem of Judea in the days of Herod the king, behold, wise men from the east came to Jerusalem. . . .

Jesse Tree Symbol & Description: Herod thought he was King of the Jews. Some of his court even thought he was the promised Messiah. They wanted Herod to free Israel from the Romans who ruled over them. But it was the Romans who had made Herod king. He was a Roman, not a Jew. He was also wicked. He craved power so much that he had some of his own sons put to death. How different Herod was from the real King of the Jews, the Lamb of God and Prince of Peace, Jesus!

Today's Song: *What Child Is This?* is an English carol written by William Chatterton Dix in 1865 and later set to the folk tune Greensleeves. Consider how, in the midst of Herod's madness, the silent Word incarnate is already pleading for our sake.

Family Reflection: Herod the Great could have been a punchline to a joke. That Herod is so Great . . .

. . . he had 2,000 bodyguards.

. . . he had three of his sons killed.

That Herod was so Great . . . he wanted people to be sad when he died, so when he was near death, he had all the most popular people in Judea arrested. He ordered that when he died, they would be executed. If his people weren't going to mourn for him, they'd at least mourn for the celebrities. (Thankfully, Herod's order to kill all Judea's celebrities upon his death was ignored.)

One more: Herod was so Great he called himself King of the Jews.

He actually was king. Rome gave him that title. Herod wasn't in David's line, he wasn't anointed by the priests as king, and he followed Jewish laws only when he felt like it.

He ruled to keep Rome happy, not God. He built a beautiful temple, but he also built temples to Roman gods. He provided for the Jewish people during famine, but he also taxed them heavily so he could send expensive gifts to his friends.

Herod wanted people to believe he was the Messiah, their true king sent by God. Although they didn't know it yet, the true King had just been placed in a manger.

Together Time: *(Discuss the following questions)*

- Who was Herod the Great? *(Herod was a king set over the Jewish people by Rome.)*
- How great was Herod?
- Do you think people today are expecting the wrong sort of Messiah? *(Discuss how we view God, as one who fulfills requests like a genie in a bottle or with a political agenda, or as one who wants to restore all creation to himself.)*

PRAYER

O Lord, grant that despite our sufferings we might keep our eyes on heaven and the glory you will reveal. Fill us with the Holy Spirit so we may learn to love and bless those who persecute us, like the first martyr, St. Stephen, who prayed for his murderers. O Jesus, who stand at the right hand of God, be with all who suffer for you. Amen.

—*Adapted from* Household Prayer, *P. G. Medd, 1864*

CELEBRATE
ST. STEPHEN'S DAY

Late one December evening in the year 415, old Lucien the priest dozed in his church.

"Lucien, Lucien, Lucien," came a voice.

Lucien shifted, opening his eyes. He sat up quickly, blinking. An elderly man stood before him and told him to go to Jerusalem, thirty miles away, and open a certain tomb.

Lucien did as directed, and uncovered the tomb of St. Stephen, which had been lost for almost four hundred years.

Nearly four hundred years earlier, around the year 35, Stephen walked those Jerusalem streets serving the poor as one of the first deacons of the early church.

Most days he likely visited widows, bringing them comfort and food from the church; he healed the sick and cast out demons; he also stepped into synagogues where his Jewish brothers and sisters worshiped. He told them their long wait was over—Jesus the Messiah had come to save them all! Many, including numerous Jewish priests, believed in Jesus.

Stephen became famous for his knowledge and sound arguments. In one synagogue, scholars from across the region, schooled in the thought of Socrates, Plato, and Aristotle, challenged him to a battle—a debate of words about Jesus.

His spirit and knowledge shone like bright stars, his words like rays of light, and his opponents left embarrassed. They seethed in anger. They would punish this arrogant man, Stephen, for making their great wisdom look like foolishness.

They enlisted friends as accomplices, men who agreed to lie about Stephen and the things he preached. They and these witnesses took their lies to the Sanhedrin.

According to one legend, while Stephen hid in the bushes from his enemies, a tiny wren, smallest of birds, chattered so loudly that the angry scribes and elders discovered him. Stephen was captured and brought before the council. His enemies shouted their charges, but Stephen sat calmly, his face like that of an angel.

And when he at last was allowed to speak, he spoke truth, he spoke light, and he spoke challenges. To the anger of those assembled, he accused, "You who received the law as delivered by angels and did not keep it!" (Acts 7:53).

As the people and elders shouted, Stephen gazed into the distance, his eyes aglow with wonder. A vision appeared to him, that of Jesus standing beside God the Father!

When he spoke of the vision, his enemies screamed and plugged their ears. They dragged him out of the city and stoned him.

Some stories say the rocks seemed to fall around Stephen as lightly as snow.

Before joining Jesus, Stephen cried out in a loud voice, "Lord, do not hold this sin against them." Even as his enemies killed him, he prayed for their forgiveness.

Share Care Packages

Care Packages remind us of St. Stephen's role as one of the church's first deacons, charged with distributing aid to those in need. St. Stephen's Day is also Boxing Day when gifts are given to those in positions of service. Assemble and deliver several care packages to neighbors, nursing home residents, college students, church staff, or others in your community who could use encouragement.

Supplies:

- baskets, gift boxes, or bags of various sizes (thrift stores are a great source for baskets!)
- gifts for the basket based on your theme
- a St. Stephen's Day note (written or printed from the Joy of Advent website)
- ribbon or decorations as desired

Care Package Recipes:

The College Package—snacks, comfortable socks, personal care items, and writing utensils.

Self-Care Package—comfortable socks, personal care items, lotions and soaps.

Family Fun Package—a puzzle or game and hot cocoa packets.

The Reader's Package—books or magazines, tea, and a mug.

Tasty Treats Package—homemade cookies and holiday plates or napkins.

Family Holiday Package—a copy of *The Joy of Advent* and an ornament!

To Do:

- Print or write a note for each basket.
- Fill with goodies.
- Deliver, anonymously if possible.

Tiny Tot Tip: Allow toddlers to help fill and deliver baskets, and have a pretend "care package" delivery at home for favorite toys.

DECEMBER 27, THIRD DAY OF CHRISTMAS

FROM THE EAST

Prepare Your Heart

(Teens & Adults)

Scripture: Matthew 2:1–10

Personal Reflection: Imagine a great caravan arriving at Herod's fortress-palace. Camels knelt, travel-worn servants adjusted packs and loitered outside as the kings had their audience with Herod. If we were watching from the gate, we might have seen the kings, faces glowing with joy, robes fluttering as they raced to their mounts.

Who were these wise men, the Magi from the East, and why were they searching the skies for a star, one that would announce a *Hebrew* king?

Those closer to home might have been searching the skies had Herod not ordered the execution of all the sages of Israel when they questioned his claim as King of the Jews (c. 6 BC). This search did not come from within Israel . . . unless it did.

Recall a young prophet carried away to Babylon. His wisdom, from "the spirit of the gods" (Dan. 5:14), was so great Nebuchadnezzar set this man over Babylon's best philosophers, scientists, astronomers.

Daniel knew the prophecy, "A Star shall come out of Jacob; A Scepter shall rise out of Israel" (Num. 24:17), and Daniel himself, after a visit from the angel Gabriel, prophesied about the number of weeks before the Messiah (Dan. 9:24–27).

What if, through 600 years, the wisdom of Daniel still lived in Babylon? What if their wisest men had counted the weeks, were searching the stars, and found what had long ago been promised?

Our reading states that upon seeing the star, the kings were *overjoyed*—which could be read as one of the greatest understatements ever written. Do we share their racing-across-the-desert joy?

Celebration!

(Families)

Focus Passage: *(Read aloud)* Matthew 2:1b–2

. . . wise men from the east came to Jerusalem, saying, "Where is he who has been born king of the Jews? For we saw his star when it rose and have come to worship him."

Jesse Tree Symbol & Description: Wise scholars in the East had been studying the sky for 600 years waiting for a very special star. What did they see? When did they first spot it? Astronomers, those who study the stars now, have several guesses. Whatever they saw, it led them to Bethlehem in the land of Judah. Their first stop: King Herod. "We're looking for the baby, the King of the Jews!" they said. How do you think King Herod would respond?

Today's Song: *O Little Town of Bethlehem,* written by Phillips Brooks in 1868, was inspired by his visit to Bethlehem three years earlier. How beautiful the picture of the silent morning stars proclaiming Christ's birth, the blessing that can come to every human heart.

Family Reflection: Do we see pictures in the stars? In a game of cosmic connect-the-dots, the ancients saw constellations of bears, lions, people, and kings!

There were no crowds outside Jesus's house, no one staring and saying, "What a wondrous star!" Only wise men, Magi from the distant East watched the sky.

What was this star that only they could see?

Astronomers study the night sky. Modern astronomers know there was no comet, no supernova, no obvious display of light. This star must have been something only the Magi would see, and only if they were looking.

One modern astronomer ran models using computer simulation to show where the stars were 2,000 years ago. One bright light stood out, not a star but the planet Jupiter, called the king planet. On December 25th, 2 BC, the king planet seemingly paused in the middle of the constellation Virgo. In Latin, *virgo* means virgin.

The King paused in the belly of the Virgin!

Many other theories captivate our imaginations. Whenever we look up at the sky, we might feel awe like Abraham's at the sheer number of stars. Let's remember, too, how God moved the stars at just the right time, in just the right way to direct a caravan of kings to the King of Kings, young Jesus.

Together Time: *(Discuss the following questions)*

- Who visited Jesus, and how did they know the way? *(Wise men or Magi from the East were guided by a star.)*
- What sort of star do you imagine guided the Magi? *(Answers will vary. Discuss different theories and even the Eastern Christian belief that the star was not a physical star but a supernatural event.)*
- Do you ever wonder whether God is in control of your life? How might this story impact that belief?

PRAYER

Merciful Lord, we ask you to cast your bright beams of light upon your church. Teach us through the writings of the apostle and evangelist St. John so we may walk in the light of your truth and gain the light of everlasting life, through Jesus Christ, our Lord. Amen.

—Adapted from Household Prayer, *P. G. Medd, 1864*

DECEMBER 28, FOURTH DAY OF CHRISTMAS

HEROD'S ENVY

Prepare Your Heart

(Teens & Adults)

Scripture: Matthew 2:7–12, 16–18

Personal Reflection: Have we lost the joy of children? Our modern world is growing hostile to children with birth rates around the world plummeting, and children are often depicted as inconveniences, luxury goods, something to be limited, afforded, planned, or avoided altogether.

Yet our very Savior came into this world as an infant.

Scholars often mark Herod's decree against Bethlehem's infant sons as a myth, a creative invention of Matthew.

We might think ancients upheld their newborn heirs as gifts and treasures, but their view was not so far off from our own modern-day culture. While Romans did celebrate a baby's birth, as ancient birth announcements attest, they also left unwanted infants outside town to die from the elements or to be killed by wild animals. Romans did not consider newborns fully human, rather these pre-humans gained humanity as they developed.

So was Herod's slaughter creative license by Matthew to show Herod's zeal for power? Since the decree was limited to boys under age two in the small village of Bethlehem and surrounding farms, scholars agree that fewer than a dozen infants were put to death.

A few "pre-humans" dying in a small, insignificant village outside the metropolis of Jerusalem would hardly be worth noting to historians of the day, not when Herod's palace was a center of murder, mania, and madness.

As we reflect on the horror of Herod's act, let us also rediscover the delight God intended to give us through children, whether by birth or adoption, and the life-giving plan he put in place when he told Adam and Eve to multiply and subdue the earth, and Abram that his descendants would outnumber the stars in the sky.

Today is the Feast of the Holy Innocents. **See page 141.**

Celebration!

(Families)

Focus Passage: *(Read aloud)* Matthew 2:16

Then Herod, when he saw that he had been tricked by the wise men, became furious, and he sent and killed all the male children in Bethlehem and in all that region who were two years old or under, according to the time that he had ascertained from the wise men.

Jesse Tree Symbol & Description: Herod thought he was King of the Jews. He would not allow anyone else to steal his kingdom! He sent the wise men off to find this king-baby for him, but the wise men did not return. So Herod did the one thing that would assure no babies in Bethlehem would ever grow up to steal his crown—he ordered all infant boys age two or younger killed. Today we remember that children are God's workmanship, knit beautifully with threads of love, imagination, and purpose.

Today's Song: *Coventry Carol* was originally performed as part of a play in Coventry, England, as early as the 1390s. It takes the form of a lullaby sung to the victims of Herod's massacre. We remember the suffering of "Rachel weeping for her children" (Jer. 31:15; Matt. 2:18), of Christ's first martyrs.

Family Reflection: The great King Herod leaned forward, gripping his robes in white-knuckled terror and rage at the words of these foreign kings. He smiled, pretending, always pretending, and said with his poison-tipped tongue, "Go and search diligently for the child, and when you have found him, bring me word, that I too may come and worship him."

And as the Magi left, he began to plot.

Herod killed everyone who threatened him. If even the whisper of a plot reached his ears, true or not, his sword swiped broadly, taking down everyone, whether friends, relatives, or his own sons.

Another king, many long generations ago, had had a similar fear. He was king over a nuisance people, useful only for the work they could do. Pharaoh saw their growing number; he knew Hebrew babies grew up to be men, and men could form armies, and armies could rebel against a king.

Pharaoh ordered baby boys to be thrown in the River Nile, and likewise Herod, in his madness, ordered all baby boys in Bethlehem killed.

In each story only one baby would escape.

The story of Moses who freed the people from Egypt was a whisper, growing louder over hundreds of years, until the new Moses came, Jesus, who would free all.

Together Time: *(Discuss the following questions)*

- What did Herod do? *(He ordered all baby boys under two years of age to be killed because he was trying to kill Jesus.)*
- Why was Herod afraid of a baby? *(He called himself King of the Jews, but the Magi said a new king had just been born. A new king could take his kingdom away.)*
- How do you demonstrate the value of all life God has created?

PRAYER

O Almighty God, who made infants glorify you by their deaths, these first martyrs. Kill all evil in us, and so strengthen us by your grace, that by the innocence of our lives we will be faithful to you even unto death. We glorify your holy name, through Jesus Christ our Lord. Amen.

—Adapted from Household Prayer, *P. G. Medd, 1864*

CELEBRATE
THE FEAST OF THE HOLY INNOCENTS

Outside the stable, stars twinkled softly. Inside, animals stood watch as silver moonlight gleamed across their shaggy coats. A young woman knelt beside a manger, unwilling to pull her finger from her newborn son's sleeping grasp.

In a year's time or perhaps a bit more—the exact time is unknown—mothers in Bethlehem might hide in that same inn's stable. They might hush their children, mouthing silent prayers that Herod's soldiers would pass them by.

On that later night, in the same village where Jesus, the Prince of Peace, first slept, terror reigned. No boy aged two or under escaped, and weeping rose to heaven like smoke wisping from snuffed candles.

How can we celebrate such sorrow?

Imagine again the cradle of Jesus. Outside, stars twinkle, and within, animals doze. Mary and Joseph perhaps pray together quietly as Jesus kicks against his cushion of straw.

Now picture a figure standing beside the cradle, a man, his profile caught in a beam of silver moonlight. St. Stephen holds the rocks of his martyrdom in his hand. He smiles at the Christ child and lays his stones, heated by his faith, at the baby's feet to warm them.

Around the crib stand children dressed in snow-white robes and wearing crowns of blossoming laurels. They wave palm branches as they sing their King a lullaby.

This is the view from heaven, outside time and place. All of Christ's work is already done, and now we have only to witness. Stephen's "Courage and Fidelity first led us to the Crib; Innocence now comes, and bids us tarry there" (Dom Guéranger, *The Liturgical Year, Christmas*, Vol. 1, 310).

Let us all tarry and watch with the shepherds over baby Jesus. Let us listen to the choir of little children singing his praises. And let us hear the words Jesus would later speak, "Let the little children come to me and do not hinder them, for to such belongs the kingdom of heaven" (Matt. 19:14).

Today we celebrate the Innocents, called the *Flowers of the Martyrs*, those who committed no crimes, did nothing to deserve Herod's hatred, yet died for the sake of Christ. "We, who have been baptized by water, should be all the more ready to honor these Little Ones, who were baptized in their own blood. . . . Truly, these tender Lambs deserve to be for ever with the Lamb of God!" (Dom Guéranger, *Christmas*, Vol. 1, 312).

Children's Pudding and Blessings

The Feast of the Holy Innocents is traditionally a Children's Day when children might be crowned kings and queens, the youngest decides activities, and special blessings are prayed. One tradition involves a Mediterranean dessert of rice pudding (reminiscent of baby food) with a berry topping to symbolize the innocent blood shed by Herod. As you enjoy this dessert, share prayers of blessing and protection over your children and children everywhere.

Pudding Recipe:
1/2 cup Basmati rice
1 can of full-fat coconut milk (or 1 1/2 cups half-and-half)
2 cups water (or 2 cups milk)
2 whole cloves
1 stick cinnamon
optional: 2 cardamom pods or 1 star anise
1/4 cups sugar
1 teaspoon vanilla extract
dash salt

Berry Sauce:
1 cup fresh or frozen raspberries, strawberries, or mixed berries
2 tablespoons sugar
optional: 1 teaspoon corn starch dissolved in 1 tablespoon of cold water

To Do:

- For the rice: Combine the rice, coconut milk, water, cloves, and cinnamon stick. Bring to a gentle boil and cook, stirring frequently, until rice is tender and much of the liquid is absorbed (about 20 minutes).
- Remove from heat, discarding cinnamon stick and cloves. Stir in sugar, vanilla, and salt.
- Serve warm or chilled in individual ramekins or small bowls.
- For the berry sauce: combine the berries and sugar and heat until bubbly and broken down. If you would like a smooth sauce, press through a mesh sieve with a rubber spatula. If the sauce is thin, add cornstarch dissolved in water and bring to a boil.
- To serve: Top individual portions with berry sauce and remember the sweetness of heaven that awaited the poor innocents!

Blessings: Placing a hand on each child's head, read one of the Scriptural blessings listed. If your home lacks children this year, pray for all the fragile and innocent in our world today.

Scriptural Blessings: Numbers 6:24–26; 1 Thessalonians 5:23–24; Ephesians 3:17b–19; Philippians 1:9–11.

Tiny Tot Tip: Little ones will enjoy a serving of their own pudding and blessing. Consider adding a nightly blessing to their bedtime routine. Make the sign of the cross on their foreheads and say a shortened form of the Aaronic blessing, "May the Lord bless you and keep you, make his face shine upon you, and give you peace. Amen."

DECEMBER 29, FIFTH DAY OF CHRISTMAS

JOSEPH'S DREAM

Prepare Your Heart

(Teens & Adults)

Scripture: Matthew 2:13–15, 19–23

Personal Reflection: Although classical artwork often paints Joseph as an elderly man, a tradition begun to combat an early heresy, he was more likely only a few years older than his wife. More important is how Joseph is God's picture of fatherhood.

Joseph's loving compassion and his forgiveness are painted in broad brushstrokes in his intention to sever the marriage contract quietly, not insisting on justice for Mary's apparent adultery. His obedience swirls onto the canvas through his unhesitating response to his first divine dream when he took Mary as his wife.

Picture the brushstrokes of faithfulness and servanthood as Joseph worked as a carpenter to support his young family with the sweat of his brow and blisters of his hands, the same hands that with gentleness guided Jesus as he taught him the family trade.

See the daubs of selflessness when Joseph left home and vocation to travel the rough roads to Egypt, and of courage as he covered more than 400 bandit-ridden, desert miles without complaint.

Notice the fine outline of leadership—God came to Joseph with these dreams, not to Mary. Joseph was charged with the responsibility of leading his family, and like Abram before him, he acted.

With Joseph we're given a portrait of fatherhood, of a true man of God. Although Joseph had already legitimized Jesus, let us remember God's words about Adam, "It is not good that the man should be alone; I will make him a helper fit for him" (Gen. 2:18). Joseph completed the Holy Family, as Christ completes the Church . . . or a restless human heart.

Celebration!

(Families)

Focus Passage: *(Read aloud)* Matthew 2:13–14

. . . behold, an angel of the Lord appeared to Joseph in a dream and said, "Rise, take the child and his mother, and flee to Egypt, and remain there until I tell you, for Herod is about to search for the child, to destroy him." And he rose and took the child and his mother by night and departed to Egypt.

Jesse Tree Symbol & Description: Imagine Joseph, tossing in his sleep, blanket held tight in his fist. His dream turned to terror, to warning. Imagine him waking, blinking into the darkness. Did he want to blink away the dream? *It was just a nightmare, go back to sleep.* Picture him waking Mary, likely beside him with young Jesus curled against her. "Mary, Mary, get up. We must go. Hurry!" And so, God saved Jesus from Herod's murder because his foster father trusted the God of dreams.

Today's Song: *I Wonder as I Wander* is an American folk tune written by John Jacob Niles in 1933 based on the haunting melody sung by an Appalachian girl, Annie Morgan. We ponder together what thoughts, fears, and wonderings overtook Mary and Joseph as they wandered the road to Egypt.

Family Reflection: Joseph, Jesus's foster father, believed in dreams. He took Mary as his wife, and now he shook her awake, helped her gather their things, and in the darkness of night, fled to Egypt, the land of God's choosing. All for a dream.

Another Joseph long before this one also believed in dreams.

This earlier Joseph was also taken to Egypt. We remember his story, his magnificent coat, and how God used him to save the future nation of Israel.

The second Joseph was sent to Egypt, and he was used to save young Jesus, the King of Kings over the whole kingdom of God.

The two Josephs, separated by so many generations, share something else—the names of their fathers. The first Joseph was son of Jacob and Rachel. The second Joseph's father is also named Jacob. And when Scripture tells of Herod's horrible murder, of a mother "weeping for her children" (Jer. 31:15; Matt. 2:18), the name used is Rachel.

The Bible records no spoken words of Mary's husband, Joseph. We see only his faith and his obedience. Perhaps his silence reflects the silence in his heart, an internal quiet that allowed him to hear and believe God's message in his dreams.

Together Time: *(Discuss the following questions)*

- What did Joseph dream? What did he do? *(God told Joseph to go to Egypt in a dream and Joseph obeyed.)*
- Do you remember the Old Testament Joseph and his coat of many colors? How was his story similar to the New Testament Joseph's? *(Answers will vary. Discuss how both Josephs had a father named Jacob and were used to help save God's people.)*
- Has God ever directed you through a dream? *(Talk about dreams and stillness, how God's voice is heard in a whisper.)*

PRAYER

O Lord, you command me to ask; grant that I may receive what you give. You have told me to seek; let me be happy in finding. You have bidden me to knock; I pray, open for me. Graciously direct and govern all my thoughts and actions, that, for the future, I may serve you and entirely devote myself to obeying you. Accept me, and draw me to yourself, that I may henceforth be yours by obedience and love, since I am already yours, as your creature: yours, O Lord, you who live and reign forever and ever. Amen.

—Adapted from St. Augustine (354–430)

DECEMBER 30, SIXTH DAY OF CHRISTMAS

BABY JOHN

Prepare Your Heart

(Teens & Adults)

Scripture: Luke 1:57–66

Personal Reflection: If we read beyond the selection of Scripture above, Zechariah's prophecy is followed by the words, "So the child grew and became strong in spirit, and was in the deserts till the day of his manifestation to Israel" (Lk. 1:80, NKJV). Notice that the child mentioned here, John the Baptist, goes into the desert. Deserts are often seen in the Bible as places of wandering, waiting, preparing, testing.

Moses led his people into the desert, and before him Abraham left his homeland and crossed desolate, unknown places in obedience to God's word.

A desert is lonely, desolate. It is also quiet. Consider how Zechariah's time of waiting for his son's birth and his son's preparation were both characterized by silence. What a beautiful contrast to John's future ministry, as a "voice crying in the wilderness" (Isa. 40:3), sharing the news as Zechariah prophesied,

> *"And you, child, will be called the prophet of the Highest . . .*
> *To give knowledge of salvation to His people*
> *By the remission of their sins."* (Lk. 1:76–77)

Consider, as well, that as John lived in desolate places, he grew *strong in spirit.* The Greek word used *pneumati* means Holy Spirit, the same spirit translated from *ru'ah* in the Old Testament. How true that the Holy Spirit most often meets us in silence and is heard most clearly in our desolation.

As we near the end of this calendar year, do we need to find a quiet space so we can better hear the Holy Spirit's voice?

Celebration!

(Families)

Focus Passage: *(Read aloud)* Luke 1:61–64

And [Elizabeth's family] said to her, "None of your relatives is called by this name." And they made signs to his father, inquiring what he wanted him to be called. And he asked for a writing tablet and wrote, "His name is John." And they all wondered. And immediately his mouth was opened and his tongue loosed, and he spoke, blessing God.

Jesse Tree Symbol & Description: Zechariah had not said a word in nine months. Finally, finally, the day had come—his first and only son would be named. The first boy in a family took his father's name in those days, but not Zechariah's son. Zechariah motioned for a tablet and for something to write with, and he wrote, "His name is John." In that moment, Zechariah's voice returned. His first words were praises to the Lord.

Today's Song: *Go Tell It on the Mountain* is an African-American spiritual first published in 1901 by John Wesley Work Jr., who recorded it from oral tradition. As we celebrate, let's think of John's future ministry, to shout in the wilderness of the world that the Savior has come.

Family Reflection: In Zechariah's day, the first son was always named after his father. The oldest son also took over his father's trade. If the father was a carpenter, the oldest son would become a carpenter. If the father was a priest, as Zechariah was, his son would become a priest.

For all of Zechariah's life, he had planned on giving his name, his wealth, and his priesthood to a son. For long years, Zechariah and Elizabeth had prayed for a son. Zechariah likely remembered God's promise to Abraham, and how Abraham and Sarah also had had a child in their old age. Maybe he had hoped for a similar promise of grandchildren and great-grandchildren to outnumber the lights in the starry sky. But just as Hannah did with Samuel, when Zechariah's son was born, he gave his child over to *God's* plan.

Zechariah's son, John the Baptist, would not marry or have children of his own. Zechariah's name would not be passed down to anyone else in his family. But God had other plans for Zechariah. His son, John, would announce the new promise, a new kingdom.

God was beginning a new family tree, one beginning with Jesus. This tree would have branches reaching to all people on earth.

Together Time: *(Discuss the following questions)*

- Why couldn't Zechariah speak? *(He was struck mute by the angel Gabriel when he questioned Gabriel's message.)*
- What was the first thing Zechariah did when he could talk again? How is this different from his response to the angel Gabriel earlier? *(Zechariah initially asked Gabriel for proof of his promise. Now Zechariah is obediently giving John the name of God's choosing.)*
- What cluttering habits could we work to get rid of to make more room for God in our minds and hearts?

PRAYER

Almighty God, to whom all hearts are open, all desires known, and from whom no secrets are hidden: cleanse the thoughts of our hearts by the inspiration of the Holy Spirit, that we may perfectly love you, and worthily magnify your holy name; through Christ our Lord. Amen.

—Prayer of Preparation,
from the Anglican Book of Common Prayer
(Renewed Ancient Text)

DECEMBER 31, SEVENTH DAY OF CHRISTMAS

THE WORD MADE FLESH

Prepare Your Heart

(Teens & Adults)

Scripture: John 1:1–5, 9–18

Personal Reflection: It was not just any well. It was Jacob's well, the very one where Jacob rolled away the covering to water Rachel's sheep—Rachel, who would become his wife.

John begins his Gospel in Genesis with creation, moves on to Jesus's words echoing Jacob's dream, ". . . you will see heaven opened, and the angels of God ascending and descending on the Son of Man" (Jn. 1:51), and soon after writes of the wedding at Cana. John the Baptist then identifies himself as the friend of the bridegroom (3:29), who is Christ, and immediately following comes the story of the woman at the well.

The woman's series of husbands is often read as sinfulness, but we're never told why each previous marriage ended. We know only that she's not a widow, so we can surmise that none of her previous husbands died. Perhaps she was like the nation of Israel trading one god for another, or she was searching for a man who would fulfill her. Perhaps the men she had married had cast her aside.

After her conversation with Jesus, she left her water jar (4:28). The clear answer was that her search was over: the Living Water had satisfied her thirst. But looking at all of John's Gospel we see Jesus the Bridegroom appearing at this well where Jacob found his wife. He was for the woman, and is for us all, the One who will never abandon nor fail to satisfy.

Celebration!

(Families)

Focus Passage: *(Read aloud)* John 1:1–5

In the beginning was the Word, and the Word was with God, and the Word was God. He was in the beginning with God. All things were made through him, and without him was not any thing made that was made. In him was life, and the life was the light of men. The light shines in the darkness, and the darkness has not overcome it.

Jesse Tree Symbol & Description: In the Bible, the book of John starts, "In the beginning was the Word." Do we remember how God made the world? He spoke with words! John writes, "And the Word became flesh and dwelt among us." The Word is Jesus, who became "flesh" or a living person. Jesus is called the Light of the World. He gives us light and hope and love. As we prepare to celebrate a new year, let's remember who is at the center of every year—and every day!

Today's Song: *Do You Hear What I Hear?* was written in 1962 by Noël Regney to music by his wife, Gloria Shayne. Originally written as a plea for peace, the song now reminds us of Jesus, the child who will bring us goodness and light.

Family Reflection: What is stronger, darkness or light?

We celebrate Jesus's birthday in the winter, when days are shortest.

Jesus's cousin John the Baptist had the special purpose of announcing Jesus's coming. John's birthday celebration is in early summer, on June 24. In the northern hemisphere, this date falls in summer, when the sun is highest in the sky and days are the longest. After John the Baptist's birthday, every day is shorter.

John the Baptist said about Jesus, "He must increase, but I must decrease" (Jn. 3:30). Amazingly, the amount of sunlight we see each day after John the Baptist's birthday decreases slowly for six long months.

Then, after the longest nights of winter, the cycle reverses.

Jesus is born, and each day the sun is a little brighter, each day just a few minutes longer.

Just as the sunlight decreased after John's birthday, it increases after Jesus's!

The Gospel of John (not John the Baptist) says Jesus was present at creation. Jesus was the Word of God. So when God said, "Let there be light," Jesus brought life and light. John later writes, "And the Word became flesh and dwelt among us."

Jesus, the Light of the World, put on a human body and brought his light and life into the world to overcome all darkness.

Together Time: *(Discuss the following questions)*

- Where was Jesus before he was born? *(Jesus has always been.)*
- What are two names for Jesus we mentioned today? *(The Word, the Light of the World.)*
- What is stronger, darkness or light? *(Answers will vary and could get quite interesting! Draw attention to John 1:5.)*

Celebration!

(Families)

Focus Passage: *(Read aloud)* Luke 2:19

But Mary treasured up all these things, pondering them in her heart.

Jesse Tree Symbol & Description: Happy New Year! Much of the world celebrates the start of a new year today. Have you ever had a treasure? What would you do with it? Most of us would put it in a safe place, from where we might take it out now and then to admire. Mary saw many people respond to her son, Jesus. The shepherds worshiped him, the Magi gave him gifts, and those in the temple said he was very important. To Mary, these memories were treasures. She put them all in her heart to keep safe and protected.

Today's Song: *The Holly and the Ivy* was first collected by musician Cecil Sharp in 1911 but reflects holly as a traditional Christmas symbol that dates back to medieval times. The song explores the plant's symbolism while referencing Mary as a sort of refrain, the repetition reminding us of how her treasured memories may have risen to conscious thought throughout Jesus's life.

Family Reflection: Picture the disciple Luke sitting with Mary, as she recounted the events of Jesus's birth. Imagine him scratching on papyrus as she spoke, capturing her words.

Perhaps Luke stopped and asked, "What do you mean, you *pondered* the shepherds' words?"

Mary would reply with a word Luke rendered in Greek as *suntéreó*. It means more than just "think about," more even than "wonder about" or "ponder."

She kept these memories carefully in her heart, protected, preserved.

She treasured them.

Jesus would grow into a toddler, then a little boy, then a bigger boy. He probably didn't seem that much different from any other child. He needed haircuts and baths, math lessons, reading and writing. But his mother, Mary, kept a treasure in her heart.

These memories lived in her heart, glowing like the flickering flames of the Lamp of God in the temple. As with a treasure of rubies or rich spices, she took her treasures out from time to time. She wondered about who this ordinary-seeming child would one day become.

When Jesus was an adult, he would tell his followers not to store up treasures on earth, but to store up treasures in heaven. Mary was the first to fill her heart with the treasure of Jesus.

Together Time: *(Discuss the following questions)*

- What did Mary keep in her heart? *(She kept treasure of the praises and prophecies about her son Jesus.)*
- How is treasuring something different from simply remembering?
- What do we find valuable enough to treasure in our hearts?

PRAYER

Holy Spirit, powerful Consoler, descend into my heart and establish in it your loving dominion. Enkindle in my tepid soul the fire of your Love so that I may be wholly subject to you. Come to me, Consoler of abandoned souls and Protector of the needy. Help the afflicted, strengthen the weak, and support the wavering. Come and purify me. Let no evil desire take possession of me. Lead me by your grace that I may always be pleasing to you. Amen.

—Adapted from St. Augustine (354–430)

CELEBRATE
THE SOLEMNITY OF MARY, MOTHER OF GOD

We all know the story of creation. On the first day God created light, on the next four days he created the whole of our magnificent world, on the sixth day he made our ancestors Adam and Eve, and on the seventh he rested.

On the eighth day, God made—

What? There is no eighth day of creation!

True, a week has only seven days. Sunday, however, is the first day of every *new* week, and Easter, also a Sunday, was the day Jesus rose from the dead. Through Jesus's death and resurrection, God healed what had broken in the first creation. In a sense, on Easter Sunday God re-created the world.

And so, in the Christmas and Easter seasons we have special celebrations called Octaves.

An octave is usually thought of as a musical term: it is the distance between two notes of the same name, one note sounding at twice or half the frequency of vibration (higher or lower pitch) of the other.

The eight days after Jesus's birth is the Octave of Christmas. This eighth day is the last note of the Octave, while Jesus's birth was the first. We celebrated Jesus's birth at the beginning of the Octave, that beautiful resonance of angels singing to shepherds. Today we celebrate the same note—God's Light coming to dwell among us—but with a different resonance. We celebrate Jesus's mother, Mary, the *Theotokos*, which is Greek for *Mother of God* or *God-Bearer*.

On this day, eight days after Jesus's birth, he was circumcised in obedience to Jewish law dating back to the time of Moses. Let us remember that in the time of Moses, God dwelled among the people in the Ark of the Covenant, which held the stone tablets of the commandments, a jar of manna from the desert, and Aaron's flowering rod signifying God's choosing of Moses and Aaron for holy service.

Today we celebrate the Ark of the New Covenant, who carried in her womb the *fulfillment* of the law, the Bread of Life for the people, and the very one who, as the new Moses, would lead us all out of slavery to sin and into the land of promise. Mary, Mother of God, carried God's very being in the person of Jesus Christ in her womb. How fitting that the new year begins with a celebration of the Mother of Jesus and all Christians!

Make "Heart of Treasure" Boxes

A tradition on John the Baptist's feast day (June 24) involves throwing away old possessions to make more room in our hearts for Christ. Instead of throwing away all the Christmas cards we received this year, we'll upcycle them into tiny treasure boxes. Fill your boxes with Bible verses, small treasures, or gifts. Keep some and gift others, or save them for packaging tiny gifts next Christmas.

Supplies:

- Christmas cards or the "Heart of Treasure" Box template from joyofadvent.com printed on heavy card stock
- scissors, pencil, ruler
- treasures: beads or plastic gems, Bible verses written on small pieces of paper

To Do:

- Print the "Heart of Treasure" Box template from joyofadvent.com
- Cut card fronts into perfect squares (by measuring or folding one corner to the inside seam). (Image A)

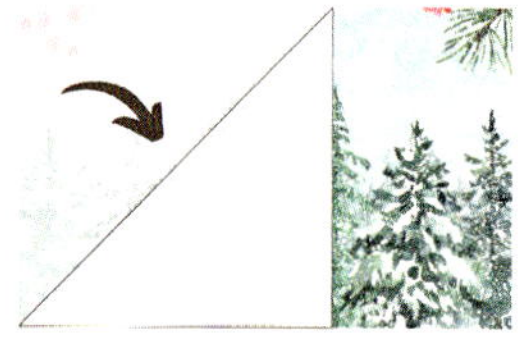

A

- Cut insides of cards into squares about 1/2 inch smaller than the fronts.
- Fold each of the corners in to meet in the center. (Image B)

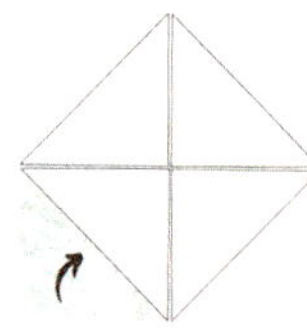

B

- Fold the straight edges inward toward the center, unfolding and repeating on the other side. (Image C)

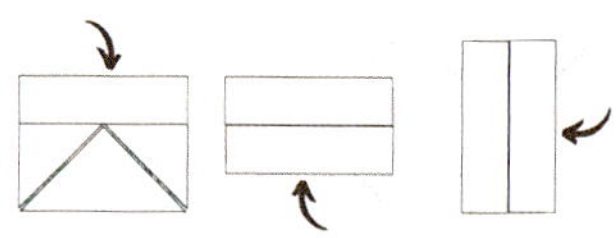

C

- Unfold completely. Your paper should look something like this. Mark along the solid lines and snip ONLY to the second fold! Cut and discard the gray triangles. (Image D)

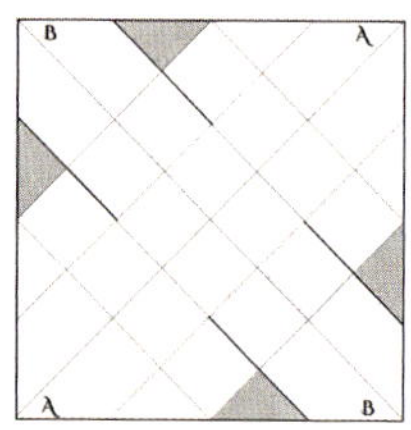

D

- 1. Refold corners A to the center. 2. Fold the snipped tabs inward to make the sides of your box. 3. Fold corners B OVER the tabs to make your box! (Image E)

E

- Fill with favorite Bible verses and treasures. Keep one as a reminder of Mary's heart filled with treasure, and give the rest away!

Tiny Tot Tip: Although folding may be tricky for little hands, toddlers will love filling and emptying their own small treasure boxes.

JANUARY 2, NINTH DAY OF CHRISTMAS

MOST PRECIOUS GIFT

Prepare Your Heart

(Teens & Adults)

Scripture: Luke 2:21–24

Personal Reflection: The privilege associated with being the oldest seems to be backward in Scripture. Esau lost his birthright, Joseph's older brothers bowed to him in desperate starvation, David's brothers stood by as their baby brother was anointed king.

The true privilege of firstborns we first see as shadows in Scripture, as if in a mirror fogged with mist. Sarah's firstborn, Isaac, was initially demanded as a sacrifice. Hannah's firstborn, Samuel, was given to the temple to serve the high priest. Moses, while not a firstborn himself, saw the firstborn of every Egyptian lose their lives.

Jesus, as firstborn, was brought to the temple after Mary's purification of thirty-three days (Lev. 12:4), to be dedicated or consecrated to the Lord. Consecrated like Samuel. Consecrated like Moses.

Ah, but Moses was not firstborn, we recall. Plus, he couldn't be consecrated—there was no tabernacle yet, no temple. Rather, Moses was placed in the water of the Nile and given over entirely to God's will. Through Moses, God saved all the firstborn of Israel from death.

Mary and Joseph, the devout couple, brought Jesus to the temple with their sacrifice of turtledoves just as tradition dictated, as if they didn't carry God enfleshed up the temple stairs. If they'd been wealthier, or had Jesus been born during lambing season, they might have brought a spotless lamb instead of birds.

Unless . . . they did bring a Lamb. After thirty-three days Mary presented her son and sacrifice to the high priest. At thirty-three years of age, Jesus would present himself, Lamb of God, as sacrifice for us all.

Celebration!

(Families)

Focus Passage: *(Read aloud)* Luke 2:22b–24

. . . [Mary and Joseph] brought [Jesus] up to Jerusalem to present him to the Lord (as it is written in the Law of the Lord, "Every male who first opens the womb shall be called holy to the Lord") and to offer a sacrifice according to what is said in the Law of the Lord, "a pair of turtledoves, or two young pigeons."

Jesse Tree Symbol & Description: Why did Mary and Joseph bring turtledoves as a sacrifice when Jesus was presented at the temple, and not a lamb? Perhaps it was not the season for lambs, or perhaps they could not afford one. Or . . . maybe they did bring a Lamb to the temple—Jesus, the Lamb of God who would one day be sacrificed to take away the sins of the whole world.

Today's Song: *Once in Royal David's City*, written as a poem by Cecil Frances Alexander, was first published in 1848 as part of a children's hymnbook. Loosely based on the Apostles' Creed, the song takes us beyond the Nativity to Jesus's childhood and "to the place where he is gone."

Family Reflection: Mary and Joseph didn't know the song *The Twelve Days of Christmas*, but when they brought Jesus to the temple, they brought two turtledoves as their sacrifice, as if they were acting out the song's second verse.

The famous Christmas song was more than a thousand years away from being written (the first printed version was published in 1780), but turtledoves were already important. When parents had a first baby, they were supposed to bring the child to the temple with a sacrifice, a gift. They could bring a lamb or a pair of birds.

Turtledoves are fascinating birds. They pick a mate and stay together for life. They build a nest together and raise their young together. Only about fifteen other species of bird mate for life.

Doves also appear often in the Bible. Noah sent a dove to look for dry land, and the Holy Spirit, the third person of the Trinity, came to earth in the form of a dove several times.

Imagine Joseph giving his sacrifice to the priests.

Two doves, together for life, might show how the Father and Holy Spirit are together forever. And in Mary's arms was the second person of the Trinity, the Lamb of God.

Together Time: *(Discuss the following questions)*

- What did Mary and Joseph bring to the temple? *(They brought two turtledoves, and the Lamb of God, Jesus!)*
- Do you know why Jesus was brought to the temple? *(Answers will vary. Draw conversation to the requirement of consecrating or giving firstborn children to God.)*
- Discuss what it means to be firstborn. Does that placement give a child special privileges?

PRAYER

O God Almighty, Father of our Lord Jesus Christ, Your only begotten Son, give me a body unstained, a pure heart, a watchful mind, and an upright understanding, and the presence of Your Holy Spirit, that I may obtain and ever hold fast to an unshaken faith in Your Truth, through Jesus Christ, Your Son, our Lord; through whom be glory to You in the Holy Spirit, forever and ever. Amen.

—*Adapted from* Ancient Collects, *William Bright, 1902*

JANUARY 3, TENTH DAY OF CHRISTMAS

A HEART PIERCED

Prepare Your Heart

(Teens & Adults)

Scripture: Luke 2:22–35

Personal Reflection: Like a tapestry being woven row by row, the Holy Spirit revealed the greatest mystery of all time one slender thread at a time.

We usually focus on Simeon's long wait of faithfulness, rewarded at last, and his departing joy.

If we peer at the picture more closely, however, we see the Holy Spirit rousing Simeon that morning and sending him to the temple and revealing Christ to him. Simeon's message of prophecy, of "revelation to the Gentiles," has deep significance, but that is not the only picture in the cloth.

Simeon shares another message, another prophecy, one *for* us but not directed to anyone beyond Jesus's mother, Mary. He prophesied about *her heart*!

Months earlier the Holy Spirit spoke through Elizabeth, Mary's cousin and the mother of John the Baptist, calling her "blessed among women." And even earlier, the Holy Spirit moved *within* Mary's body to take threads of Mary and threads of God to weave, in perfect unity of humanity and divinity, the infant Jesus.

We see a divine concern for the woman who would forever be the mother of God's own Son. A concern mirrored by Jesus himself, when on the cross he told the only disciple still with him in his final moments, "Behold, your mother" (Jn. 19:27).

Yes, Simeon saw, because the Holy Spirit revealed, that the treasures stored within Mary's heart would one day spill like blood from pierced hands, feet, side. That treasure is for us all.

Celebration!

(Families)

Focus Passage: *(Read aloud)* Luke 2:34–35

And Simeon blessed them and said to Mary his mother, "Behold, this child is appointed for the fall and rising of many in Israel, and for a sign that is opposed (and a sword will pierce through your own soul also), so that thoughts from many hearts may be revealed."

Jesse Tree Symbol & Description: A very old man had been waiting at the temple for a very long time. What was Simeon waiting for? The Holy Spirit had promised that he would one day see Christ, the Messiah. When he saw Mary and Joseph with Jesus he said, ". . . my eyes have seen your salvation." He then looked at Mary and saw how her heart would be pierced. He knew that the baby in Mary's arms would have to die for the salvation of the world.

Today's Song: *Sussex Carol* was written or recorded first by Irish Bishop Luke Wadding in 1684. Imagine Simeon's rejoicing as he finally, after a lifetime of waiting, sees the Redeemer!

Family Reflection: Having a baby was perfectly ordinary.

Bringing an infant to the temple was also ordinary, so ordinary that Joseph and Mary were likely one couple in a small crowd of new parents.

It's true that Mary's pregnancy announcement was far from ordinary, and it's not every day angels appear to shepherds.

But Mary and Joseph didn't see the angels themselves, and weeks had passed since that surprising visit in the inn's stable.

And the Magi with their gifts of gold and precious herbs hadn't yet arrived (although they were on their way by now!).

Despite the extraordinary beginning of Jesus's story, by all outward appearances Mary and Joseph were parents of an ordinary baby boy.

And then one elderly man recognized the extraordinary waiting in line with all the other new parents.

God's most amazing works often hide in plain sight.

God himself became a human baby who grew into an ordinary carpenter in the eyes of the world.

Simeon would tell this seemingly ordinary mother of an extraordinary sorrow.

Her pierced heart would have an extraordinary purpose. Through it would shine Jesus, "a light for revelation to the Gentiles" (Lk. 2:32).

Together Time: *(Discuss the following questions)*

- Who was Simeon waiting for? *(The Holy Spirit told Simeon he would see the Messiah, the Savior of all.)*
- How would Mary's heart be pierced? *(Her only son would die on the cross.)*
- How does Mary's treasure become treasure for us all?

PRAYER

"Ye children, praise the Lord: praise the name of the Lord" (Ps. 113:1). We praise you, we sing hymns to you, we bless you for your great glory, O Lord our King, the Father of Christ the Lamb, who takes away the sin of the world. "Now, Lord, let your servant depart in peace, according to your word, for my eyes have seen your salvation, which you prepared before the face of all people, a light for the revelation to the Gentiles, and the glory of your people Israel" (Lk. 2:29–32).

—Adapted from the Orthodox Vespers Liturgy (c. 380): Based on the Song of Simeon

JANUARY 4, ELEVENTH DAY OF CHRISTMAS

WAITING

Prepare Your Heart

(Teens & Adults)

Scripture: Luke 2:36–40

Personal Reflection: Anna receives four sentences in Scripture, with no recorded words. We might skim by her quickly, another example of faithfulness included only to reinforce the words of prophecy and praise already spoken by Simeon.

Details are never dropped into Scripture without a purpose, including the name of Anna's father, Phanuel, of the tribe of Asher.

If we think back to the history of Israel, we'll remember that shortly after King David, the kingdom split. Ten tribes separated to become Israel and two tribes became Judah. By Anna's day, both kingdoms had long since fallen, the glory of old having passed away.

Jeremiah shared a hope for the Messiah, a promise of a "new covenant with the house of Israel and the house of Judah" (Jer. 31:31). The Messiah, the Hope of Israel, would unite the two kingdoms, joining them "in an everlasting covenant that will never be forgotten" (Jer. 50:5).

Anna's heritage was mentioned because it mattered.

Simeon, who had also been waiting for the Messiah, was either a priest of the line of Levi, or was Simeon ben Hillel, from the tribe of Benjamin. Either way, his lineage traced back to the house of Judah. Anna's father was of the house of Israel.

Four sentences show us a widow who, after her husband's death in her youth, like Israel's fall into captivity, waited for "the voice of mirth and the voice of gladness, the voice of the bridegroom" (Jer. 33:11), her bridegroom, her redeemer.

Celebration!

(Families)

Focus Passage: *(Read aloud)* Luke 2:37–38

She did not depart from the temple, worshiping with fasting and prayer night and day. And coming up at that very hour she began to give thanks to God and to speak of him to all who were waiting for the redemption of Jerusalem.

Jesse Tree Symbol & Description: Anna had been praying in the temple for more than sixty years. As soon as Jesus and his earthly parents came, she praised God and told everyone that Jesus was the Messiah they had been waiting for. He would save the people! A flower bulb waits underground all winter. When spring arrives, it sends up green leaves and bursts forth flowers. Anna's long and faithful wait became a beautiful flower when she saw Jesus in the temple.

Today's Song: *Lo, How a Rose E'er Blooming,* first sung in German in the 1400s and printed in 1599, focuses on the shoot that will spring forth from the stump of Jesse. Imagine Anna's faith as a flower coming to bloom on a cold winter night.

Family Reflection: Would we wait a year for something? How about ten years? Or fifty?

When Anna's husband died, she could have remarried. Instead she went to the temple to live and to wait, and wait, and wait.

She waited for more than sixty years.

The people were promised a Messiah, a Savior, already in Genesis after Eve's disobedience. The Hebrew people had been waiting much, much longer than sixty years—they had been waiting for thousands of years!

The Rose of Sharon (S. of S. 2:1; Isa. 35:1), wasn't like our rose with its thorny stem, nor the shrub we call the Rose of Sharon now. The Rose of Sharon was like a crocus or narcissus, its bulb left in the ground through the longest days of winter. Before spring had fully thawed the earth, the flowers bloomed, often against a backdrop of winter's last snow.

Anna's faithful wait was like that crocus.

The world had been in darkness for thousands of years, but life bloomed in the arms of Mary. The elderly widow Anna saw the Rose of Sharon, like a shoot growing from a stump, in the rosy cheeks of baby Jesus.

Together Time: *(Discuss the following questions)*

- Why was Anna waiting? *(She was waiting to see the Messiah promised to Israel.)*
- How was Anna's wait like a crocus bulb? *(Anna's wait represents the long wait of all of Israel. Like a bulb planted in fertile soil, Anna's patient wait for the promised Messiah yielded fruit.)*
- Why is it important for the two houses (Israel and Judah) to be reunited in the New Covenant? *(Because it is through this restoration among the original tribes that the Messiah, Jesus, will create a new people, new Israelites with the Gentiles, and salvation will spread to the whole world.)*

PRAYER

Above all, long-expected Messiah, do come! Your ancient people who despised you once are waiting for you in your second coming, and we, the Gentiles, who knew you not, neither regarded you, we, too, are watching for your advent. . . . The whole creation groans in pain together until now. Your own expect you; we are longing till we are weary for your coming. Come quickly, Lord Jesus, come quickly. Amen and Amen.

—Charles Spurgeon (1834–1892)

JANUARY 5, TWELFTH DAY OF CHRISTMAS

MY FATHER'S HOUSE

Prepare Your Heart

(Teens & Adults)

Scripture: Luke 2:41–52

Personal Reflection: Do we remember our child's first words? They may be written in a baby book or shared on social media, and, in a mother's heart, treasured.

Today's passage shares the first recorded words of Jesus.

His words are questions: "Why were you looking for me?" and "Did you not know . . .?" Through these words we see glimmers of Jesus's reason for joining frail humanity, his identity, and his promise. He is the Son of God the Father, come to do his Father's will, and all who seek him will find him (Jer. 29:12; Matt. 7:6).

His words have special meaning for us as we finish the season and celebration of Christmas.

Every life will face times of trial when Jesus seems far, when we might ask, "Where have you been? Why have you done this to us?"

Jesus's words will remind us that he is there, we have only to look in the right place.

We are to look in his Father's house, in the center of his will and purpose.

We may not understand the works of God, as Mary and Joseph did not understand. We may walk through valleys of silence or storm or dry bones, and we may see divine actions that we didn't anticipate. Jesus as a boy in the temple did not tell his parents where he'd gone in advance—he simply went. He expects us to follow where he leads and to seek him, the very presence of God, which is why he went to his Father's house. It is where we can always find him.

Tonight is Twelfth Night. See page 185.

Celebration!

(Families)

Focus Passage: *(Read aloud)* Luke 2:49

And he said to them, "Why were you looking for me? Did you not know that I must be in my Father's house?"

Jesse Tree Symbol & Description: What does it mean to *dwell*? To dwell means to live. The temple was where the Jewish people believed God dwelled. As Jesus stood in the temple, God was again dwelling in the temple. Think about Isaac and Abraham, who must have walked right by the thicket where the ram was waiting. The priests and people didn't know that they were speaking to Jesus, God as man. He is the final Sacrifice, the Lamb who will take away the sins of the world.

Today's Song: *Hark! The Herald Angels Sing,* based on Luke 2:14, was written by Charles Wesley and first published in 1739. Consider how Jesus "laid his glory by" as he, God incarnate, hid in plain sight in the temple.

Family Reflection: As the season of Christmas finishes, let's look back to Moses, to an item God told the people to build.

The Ark of the Covenant was a wooden box specially designed to hold three important things: the stone tablets of the ten commandments, a special rod blooming with flowers, and a bowl of manna.

The Ark of the Covenant was kept in the temple, in a room called the Holy of Holies. Young Samuel was sleeping right outside this room when he heard God's voice. God's presence dwelled or lived in the Ark of the Covenant.

When young Jesus gave reason to Mary and Joseph to worry, the Ark of the Covenant had been missing for almost 600 years, since the time of Daniel.

The Holy of Holies was empty.

When Jesus was lost for three days, the Feast of the Passover had just finished, and like a shadow of the long-missing Ark of the Covenant, he was found in the temple.

Jesus, God enfleshed, called the Bread of Life, the Shoot from the Rod of Jesse, the Word of God, filled the temple.

Together Time: *(Discuss the following questions)*

- Where did Mary and Joseph find Jesus? *(In the temple.)*
- Why was Jesus's visit to the temple important? *(The temple was God's house, or dwelling place. Jesus, God enfleshed, was dwelling again in the temple.)*
- Where do you seek Jesus?

PRAYER

Though my faults are many, my misery great, my spiritual poverty extreme, my hope in you surpasses everything. It is superior to my weakness, greater than my difficulties, stronger than death. Though temptations should assail me, I will hope in you. Though I break my resolutions, I will look to you confidently for grace to keep them at last. Though you should kill me, even then I will trust in you, for you are my Father, my God, the support of my salvation. You are my kind, compassionate, and indulgent parent, and I am your devoted child who cast myself into your arms and beg your blessing. I put my trust in you; and so trusting, I shall not be confounded. Amen.

—Providence of God by St. Claude de la Colombiere (1641–1682)

JANUARY 6

EPIPHANY

Prepare Your Heart

(Teens & Adults)

Scripture: Matthew 2:1–12

Personal Reflection: Today many of us pack away our stockings, wrap up our strings of lights and stow them all in a basement or attic to await the coming year. All but the nativity, which stays a few days more, because the Magi, having traveled so long, so far, have at last arrived at the cradle of baby Jesus.

Advent is a time of expectation, of awaiting, like the ten virgins in Jesus's parable (Matt. 25). The bridegroom is coming, and we sit at the ready in the dark of night longing for the coming of dawn and with it our Beloved. During Christmastide we rejoice at the darkness shattered, night's silence broken by a choir of angels singing, "Glory to God in the highest" (Lk. 2:14a). We celebrate as the Light of the World, fully God yet fully human, still wet from Mary's womb, takes a first, deep breath of the air he made.

Imagine the Magi gazing heavenward. Just like the star that moved across the sky, the rising dawn chased darkness around the earth, and the light of Christ glowed beyond Bethlehem, beyond the Jews awaiting the messiah. The Magi's visit demonstrates the Light of Christ brightening all the world. "Nations will come to your light, and kings to the brightness of your dawn" (Isa. 60:3, NABRE).

This is Epiphany. It is celebration, revelation, light *beyond* Bethlehem, to the Gentiles and the world. The gift of the Messiah is for all, as Paul writes in his letter to the Romans, "And again Isaiah says, 'The root of Jesse will come, even he who arises to rule the Gentiles; in him will the Gentiles hope'" (Rom. 15:12).

The kings from the East knelt before the King of the Universe, the Bridegroom, and laid wedding gifts at tiny feet that would one day be pierced. For us. Let us end this season full. Full of memories of togetherness, yes, but also full of gratitude, joy, and adoration for our King and Beloved who loved us enough to become one of us and to be our sacrifice that we may be with him as children of Adam in a new Eden.

Because we have moved out of Christmastide, there is no Family Celebration today. Complete your personal reflection with prayer, and share the Celebrate Epiphany reading and activities with the whole family.

PRAYER

Almighty and eternal God,
Brightness of faithful souls,
You brought the Gentiles to your light,
and made known to them him who is the true Light,
and the bright and morning Star.
Fill the world with your glory,
and show yourself by the radiance of your light to all nations;
through Jesus Christ our Lord. Amen.

—From the Gregorian Sacramentary, c. 900s

CELEBRATE
EPIPHANY

The Gift Revealed

Outside the house, camels rested, servants waited, and those scholars who couldn't fit inside the small house paced, their hands clasped in excitement and expectation. They gazed up at the star again and again. *Yes, this is the place!*

Inside the house, according to St. Bede the Venerable in the book *Collectanea et Flores* (735), the first of the Magi sank to his knees before the Christ child. Melchior's white hair and long gray beard spoke as much to his age as his wisdom as he opened a chest filled with gold, the gift for a king.

The second of the Magi, Caspar, then stepped forward. His beardless cheeks shone pink with youth and joy as he knelt before the Child King. He unwrapped a parcel, the fragrance of frankincense filling the senses of all in the household. This costly resin was also a gift fit for a king, but it meant so much more. The smoke it produced as incense was said to drive away serpents, and its aroma was pleasing to God when the high priest placed it on temple offerings. Jesus, just a toddler, may have leaned forward to inhale.

Baltasar, the third of the Magi, bowed low, his dark hands uncorking a jar of the most valuable and sacred oil, oil of myrrh. This, too, was a king's gift. It was gathered one drop at a time from the wounds on trunks of the thorned myrrh trees. This oil anointed kings, prophets, and priests. This oil would one day be used on Jesus's wounded body before a stone was rolled against the tomb's door (cf. Weisner, *Handbook of Christian Feasts and Customs*, 147–148).

The fragrances mingled in Mary and Joseph's humble Bethlehem house. Candlelight danced over the gold of a king as the young God-in-Flesh smiled at the sweet aroma of frankincense, and they rejoiced together in the wounding required to enjoy the oil of myrrh, for myrrh had use beyond anointing and burial—it was also a wedding oil.

The three gifts of the Magi tell the story: Gold—a gift of kings. Frankincense—a gift of divinity. Myrrh—a gift of death and of wedding joy!

Today Christmastide is over, and we celebrate the Epiphany, which means *manifestation*, or *revealing*. The Magi from the mysterious East came by God's direction to see the King of the Jews and to worship him. Jesus's person as God incarnate was revealed to the Gentiles.

We also celebrate the revelation of Jesus to all, and the Epiphany that is yet to come. One day, in an hour unknown, Jesus the Bridegroom will return for the greatest wedding banquet of all time (Rev. 19:1–9)! As we go forward into the next seasons of the year, let us all, like the Parable of the Ten Virgins (Matt. 25), keep our lamps burning and, like Simeon and Anna, never forget the reason for our wait.

Host a Twelfth Night "Gift" Exchange

Twelfth Night, the eve of Epiphany, was traditionally a time of frivolity and good-natured pranking. Host a Twelfth Night Party and hold a White Elephant Gift Exchange! Invite family, friends, neighbors, or whomever you'd most like to celebrate with. We've shared laughs at countless White Elephant Gift Exchanges over the years. Every time, however, several early gift-openers end up with gag gifts and are left to watch as the highly valued gifts are eagerly traded. It's all in fun, but to keep disappointment low (and keep children engaged and happy), we adapted the traditional rules to include more mystery and guesswork.

20 + C + M + B + XX*

* *final two digits of the current year*

Leader (while inscribing): The three Wise Men, *(write C)* Caspar, *(write M)* Melchior, *(write B)* and Baltasar followed the star to Bethlehem and the child Jesus *(write 20)* two thousand, *(write the current year)* and [current year] years ago. Christus *(write the + after the C)* Mansionem *(write the + after the M)* Benedicat *(write the + after the B)*, "May Christ bless this house" *(write the final + sign)*, and remain with us throughout the year. Amen.

All: *Recite the Lord's Prayer (Matt. 6:9b–13).* Amen.

AFTERWORD

Thank you for celebrating with *The Joy of Advent* this year! When Stephen and I were growing up, Christmas was a single day. Yes, there was anticipation—plenty of it! But we weren't raised in liturgical traditions with Advent and Christmastide. Incorporating those and the rest of the seasons of the church year into our lives has been exciting and invigorating.

Even if the church seasons are old and familiar to you, now is a time to reflect. Was your season more meaningful? List new traditions you developed, as well as ones you discovered and might want to employ in coming years. Part of the blessing of this book is its freshness.

After eleven months away, you will return with new vigor, new understanding, and renewed excitement. Over the past two decades *The Joy of Advent* (initially in a primordial form) changed our family, growing us together and growing us in our faith. We're certain it can do the same for yours.

Be sure to connect with us at our website and through social media, and consider gifting JOY next season by giving copies of *The Joy of Advent: Family Celebrations for Advent and the Twelve Days of Christmas* to those on your Christmas list.

Herrad of Landsberg (1130–1195), Hortus Deliciarum,
"Der Stammbaum Christi" (The Genealogy of Christ), ca. 1180

Hortus Deliciarum, Latin for "Garden of Delights," is a remarkable medieval manuscript compiled by Herrad of Landsberg, a twelfth-century nun and abbess of Hohenburg Abbey in present-day France. This illuminated encyclopedia, created between 1167 and 1185, serves as a comprehensive compendium of knowledge, encompassing theology, philosophy, natural history, and more. "The Genealogy of Christ" is one of the most notable sections in the encyclopedia and traces the lineage of Jesus Christ from Adam and Eve to the Virgin Mary. The genealogy serves not only as an historical record but also as a theological statement, emphasizing Christ's divine lineage and his central place within salvation history.

SCRIPTURE CREDITS

Unless otherwise noted, all Scriptures used in this book are taken from The Holy Bible, English Standard Version® (ESV®)© 2001 by Crossway, a publishing ministry of Good News Publishers. All rights reserved. The ESV text may not be quoted in any publication made available to the public by a Creative Commons license. The ESV may not be translated in whole or in part into any other language. ESV Text Edition: 2016

(The Holy Bible, English Standard Version (ESV) is adapted from the Revised Standard Version of the Bible, copyright Division of Christian Education of the National Council of the Churches of Christ in the U.S.A. All rights reserved.)

Scriptures marked KJV are taken from the King James Version of the Holy Bible.

Scripture quotations marked NABRE are taken from the *New American Bible, revised edition* © 2010, 1991, 1986, 1970 Confraternity of Christian Doctrine, Washington, D.C. and are used by permission of the copyright owner. All Rights Reserved. No part of the New American Bible may be reproduced in any form without permission in writing from the copyright owner.

Scripture quotations marked NASB taken from the (NASB®) New American Standard Bible®, Copyright © 1960, 1971, 1977, 1995, 2020 by The Lockman Foundation. Used by permission. All rights reserved. lockman.org

Scripture quotations marked NCB are taken from THE NEW CATHOLIC BIBLE®. Copyright © 2019 Catholic Book Publishing Corp. Used by permission. All rights reserved.

Scripture quotations marked NIV are taken from the Holy Bible, New International Version®, NIV®. Copyright © 1973, 1978, 1984, 2011 by Biblica, Inc.® Used by permission of Zondervan. All rights reserved worldwide. www.zondervan.com The "NIV" and "New International Version" are trademarks registered in the United States Patent and Trademark Office by Biblica, Inc.®

Scripture quotations marked NKJV are taken from the New King James Version®. Copyright © 1982 by Thomas Nelson. Used by permission. All rights reserved.

Scripture quotations marked NRSVue are taken from the New Revised Standard Version Updated Edition. Copyright © 2021 National Council of Churches of Christ in the United States of America. Used by permission. All rights reserved worldwide.

RESOURCES

Anglican Church in North America. *Book of Common Prayer and Administration of the Sacraments*. Huntington Beach, CA.: Anglican Liturgy Press, 2019.

Bright, William. *Ancient Collects and Other Prayers Selected for Devotional Use from Various Rituals*. 8th ed. London: Parker & Co., 1902.

Brunner, Bernd. *Inventing the Christmas Tree*. Translated by Benjamin A. Smith. New Haven: Yale University Press, 2012.

Charles, R. H. "The Book of Jubilees." *The Apocrypha and Pseudepigrapha of the Old Testament*. Oxford, UK: Clarendon Press, 1913.

Guéranger, Dom Prosper. *The Liturgical Year. Advent*. 2d ed. Translated by Dom Laurence Shepherd. London: Burns & Oates, etc., 1870.

Guéranger, Dom Prosper. *The Liturgical Year. Christmas*. Vols. 1 & 2. 3d ed. Translated by Dom Laurence Shepherd. London: Burns & Oates, etc., 1904.

Hayes-Williams, Jean Anne. "The Earliest Dated Tree of Jesse Image: Thematically Reconsidered." *Athanor* 18 (2000): 17–23.

Irenaeus of Lyons, St. *Against Heresies. The Ante-Nicene Fathers: The Writings of the Fathers Down to A.D. 325*. Volume I. Edited by Alexander Roberts and James Donaldson. Buffalo, NY: The Christian Literature Publishing Company, 1885.

Joy of Advent Website: joyofadvent.com

Medd, P. G. *Household Prayer from Ancient and Authorized Sources*. London: Rivingtons, 1864.

Staley, Vernon. *The Liturgical Year: An Explanation of the Origin, History & Significance of the Festival Days & Fasting Days of the English Church*. London: A. R. Mowbray & Co., 1907.

Weiser, Francis X. *Handbook of Christian Feasts and Customs: The Year of the Lord in Liturgy and Folklore*. New York: Harcourt, Brace and Company, 1958.

Weiser, Francis X. *Religious Customs in the Family: The Radiation of Liturgy into Christian Homes*. Collegeville, MN: Liturgical Press, 1956.

Weiser, Francis X. *The Christmas Book*. New York: Harcourt, Brace and Company, 1952.

ABOUT THE AUTHORS

Rebecca Grabill has been writing since childhood, her first book about a kitten published between homemade cardboard covers in second grade. Although she studied religion and philosophy in university, she continued writing, earning an MFA from Hamline University and publishing multiple picture books (no longer with homemade covers) and a collection of poetry with a variety of New York and independent publishers. She has also published a wide array of fiction, essays, and poetry in magazines and journals and photographs for Getty Images. She balances writing with homeschooling the younger of her six children, launching her young adults, church activities, and overseeing a small flock of chickens in rural West Michigan.

Stephen Grabill has been steeped in all things theology and economics for more than three decades, earning a PhD in Systematic Theology and Moral Theology, then writing, editing, speaking, and making films in an academic and think tank setting for almost twenty years. He then followed the Spirit's leading to shift careers, focusing his energies on a tech startup, Moja Market LLC, whose mission is to promote human flourishing and economic development in Sub-Saharan Africa. He now directs Moja's educational efforts while consulting, co-authoring with his wife Rebecca, supporting his home church, St. Isidore the Laborer in Grand Rapids, Michigan, and leading his family of eight into always new and exciting territory.

Clare Therese Gray is an illustrator, author, and designer based in the UK. Her work is inspired by the natural environment of her rural Hampshire surroundings, where she lives and works on a farm with her husband and young family. Trained at the Royal Drawing School, she makes traditional techniques central to her work in a variety of mixed media including gouache, watercolor, pencil, and ink. Her experience spans a range of clients and sectors from textiles to craft collections, homewares to book illustration. She authored *Painting Nature with Clare* and *Woodland Watercolor: A Coloring Workbook*, and illustrated the *Agnes Series* picture books for children. She shares her unique painting and drawing style on her Instagram account @claretheresegray.

ABOUT PARACLETE PRESS

Paraclete Press is the publishing arm of the Cape Cod Benedictine community, the Community of Jesus. Presenting a full expression of Christian belief and practice, we reflect the ecumenical charism of the Community and its dedication to sacred music, the fine arts, and the written word.

SCAN TO READ MORE

ALSO AVAILABLE

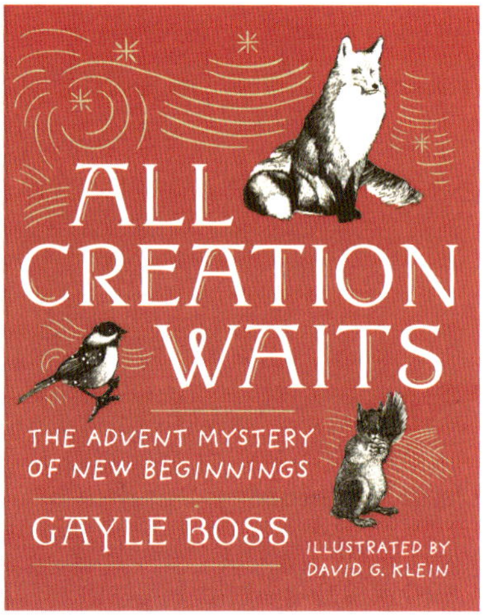

WWW.PARACLETEPRESS.COM